Praise for *Grieving: Dispatches from (*

"A lucid, poignant collection of essays and p~...,
to writing itself, and to the power of language." —*New York Times
Book Review*

"A concise but weighty and timely collection of essays and dispatches." —*Washington Post*

"If the continuation of violence depends on silence and impunity,
Rivera Garza believes that writing can throw a wrench in that
machine." —*The Nation*

"Imbued with optimism and an activist's passion for reshaping the
world." —*The New Yorker*

"Highlighting activists and social movements, *Grieving* is a
thought-provoking, moving analysis of social and political reckoning in Mexico." —*Booklist*

"A riveting collection of essays. . . . The book succeeds in shedding
light on the dynamics of state power, patriarchy, and violence,
allowing femicide to exist and the counterresponse 'tragic agency'
to emerge." —*Latino Book Review*

"A powerful, heartbreaking chronicle of the violence that's taken
place in Mexico along the US-Mexico border. . . . Not only a book
of mourning and loss, but one of vitality, of love, and of hope for a
changed future." —**Refinery29**

"Rivera Garza applies a lingual scalpel to the narrative of systemic
violence: a narrative enacted on both sides of the border by governments, law enforcement, drug cartels, and the media who sensationalize, erase, or ignore the violence." —*Brooklyn Rail*

"A compelling work of social criticism that speaks to a desperate
time." —*Kirkus Reviews*

"[*Grieving*] is a new texture, a different, completely ethical reading contract produced by means of slowness, evincing a corporate, capitalist, neoliberal political system that bet on monetary profit rather than our bodies. These fragments take on a life of their own in this book. They are reorganized in the form of a map, a new reality in which we all exist." —*Latin American Literature Today*

"*Grieving* is a major reckoning with violence in contemporary Mexico, and its relevance, like the causes of the crisis, extends far beyond the border. A brilliant work." —**Rubén Martínez, *Crossing Over***

"A bold, luminous collection from Mexico's most impressive essayist and writer." —**Lina Meruane, *Seeing Red***

"At once a gorgeous elegy, a clarion call to action, and a revindication of the human spirit. Rivera Garza's prose, and her political celebration of the written word, is liberatory." —**John Washington, *The Dispossessed***

"Laying bare the foundations of state violence and collective trauma, while also imploring its readers to imagine the world we want to live in, *Grieving* is the perfect book to accompany us through these uncertain times." —**Rosa Alcalá, *Undocumentaries***

"Sarah Booker's translation recreates the urgency of Rivera Garza's prose with exceptional vitality." —**Idra Novey, *Those Who Knew***

"*Grieving* documents and shares a writer's struggle to face the horror enveloping her country, and the world, with every possible tool and weapon of both language and feeling. The result is a vital and burning work of social grieving; that is, of fighting back, of not giving up or giving in, of commitment and survival." —**John Gibler, *I Couldn't Even Imagine That They Would Kill Us***

"Cristina Rivera Garza writes about the universal conditions of our world today. She does so with prose unmatched for its sharp intelligence, poetry, clarity, empathy, liveliness, passion. She is a genius, 'our' necessary voice." —**Francisco Goldman, *The Interior Circuit***

GRIEVING

Dispatches from a Wounded Country

Cristina Rivera Garza

TRANSLATED FROM THE SPANISH
BY SARAH BOOKER

THE FEMINIST PRESS
AT THE CITY UNIVERSITY OF NEW YORK
NEW YORK CITY

Published in 2020 by the Feminist Press
at the City University of New York
The Graduate Center
365 Fifth Avenue, Suite 5406
New York, NY 10016

feministpress.org

First Feminist Press edition 2020

 This book was made possible thanks to a grant from New York State
Council on the Arts with the support of Governor
Andrew M. Cuomo and the New York State Legislature.

Second printing March 2021

Cover design by Sukruti Anah Staneley
Text design by Drew Stevens

Library of Congress Cataloging-in-Publication Data
Names: Rivera Garza, Cristina, 1964- author. | Booker, Sarah, translator.
Title: Grieving : dispatches from a wounded country / Cristina Rivera Garza
  ; translated from the Spanish by Sarah Booker.
Description: First Feminist Press edition. | New York, NY : Feminist Press,
  2020. | Includes bibliographical references.
Identifiers: LCCN 2020026940 (print) | LCCN 2020026941 (ebook) | ISBN
  9781936932931 (paperback) | ISBN 9781936932948 (ebook)
Subjects: LCSH: Rivera Garza, Cristina, 1964—Translations into English. |
  Mexico—Social conditions—21st century—Translations into English.
Classification: LCC PQ7298.28.I8982 A2 2011 (print) | LCC PQ7298.28.I8982
  (ebook) | DDC 868/.703—dc23
LC record available at https://lccn.loc.gov/2020026940
LC ebook record available at https://lccn.loc.gov/2020026941

Contents

Under the Narco Sky

Writing as We Grieve, Grieving as We Write

Taking Shelter: Horror, the State, and Social Suffering in Twenty-First-Century Mexico

On September 14, 2011, we awoke once again to the image of two bodies hanging from a bridge. One man, one woman. He, tied by the hands. She, by the wrists and ankles. Just like so many other similar occurrences, and as noted in newspaper articles with a certain amount of trepidation, the bodies showed signs of torture. Entrails erupted from the woman's abdomen, opened in three different places.

It is hard to write about these atrocities. In fact, the very reason acts like these are carried out is so that they render us speechless. The ultimate goal of horror is to completely paralyze us, to render us utterly powerless, to disfigure our bodies beyond recognition—an offense not only against human life but also, above all, against the human condition.

In *Horrorism: Naming Contemporary Violence*—an indispensable book for thinking through this reality, as understanding it is almost impossible—Adriana Cavarero reminds us that terror manifests when the body trembles and flees in order to survive.[1] The terrorized body experiences fear, and upon finding itself within fear's grasp, attempts to escape it. Meanwhile, horror, taken from the Latin verb *horrere*, goes far beyond the fear that so frequently alerts us to danger or threatens to transcend it. Confronted with Medusa's decapitated head, a body destroyed beyond human recognition, we, the horrified, part our lips and, incapable of uttering a single word, incapable of articulating the disarticulation that fills our gaze, mouth wordlessly. Horror is intrinsically linked to repugnance, Cavarero argues. Bewildered and immobile, we are stripped of our agency, frozen in a scene of everlasting marble statues. We stare, and even though we stare fixedly, or perhaps precisely *because* we stare fixedly, we cannot do anything. More than vulnerable—a condition we all experience—we, the horrified, are defenseless. More than fragile, we are helpless. As such, horror is, above all, a spectacle—the most extreme spectacle of power.

What we Mexicans have been forced to witness at the beginning of the twenty-first century—on the streets, on pedestrian bridges, on television, or in the papers—is, without a doubt, one of the most chilling spectacles of contemporary horror. Bodies sliced open from end to end, chopped into unrecognizable pieces, left on the streets. Bodies exhumed in a state of decay from hundreds upon hundreds of mass graves. Bodies tossed from pickup trucks onto crowded streets. Bodies burned on enormous pyres. Bodies without hands or without ears or without noses. Disappeared bodies, unable to claim their suitcases from the bus stations where their belongings have arrived. Persecuted bodies, bodies without air, bodies without fingernails or eyelashes. This is the very essence of horror. This is a more current version of a kind of modern horror that has shown its atrocious face in Armenia, in Auschwitz, in Kosovo.

In the case of Mexico at the end of the twentieth century and beginning of the twenty-first, horror is intimately tied to a misnamed war—the military conflict escalated by President Felipe Calderón in 2006 as he tried to legitimize a highly contested election victory. It has been called, and still is, the drug war, the war on drugs; but we know other, more truthful names: the war against the Mexican people, the war against women. The war against the rest of us. While this state of siege may have become more visible after the 2006 elections, the war as such actually began decades earlier. Historian Adela Cedillo persuasively argues that there is a link between the Mexican dirty war unleashed in the 1970s against those designated enemies of the state and the emergence of drug lords who became accomplices, when not directly participating, in counterinsurgent strategies designed to reinforce the hegemony of the Partido Revolucionario Institucional (PRI), in power since 1929.[2] Indeed, the first drug war was waged in Mexico, and it all began in the Golden Quadrilateral region comprised of the states Chihuahua, Sonora, Sinaloa, and Durango. Right there, in neglected areas of Mexico with little state presence, violence was used against the poor, especially against the rural poor who had responded favorably to, or had organized themselves into, guerilla movements, such as the 23rd of September Communist League. Secret Service documents attest that the PRI machine reacted quickly and massively against any kind of participants of social mobilization, generously employing counterinsurgent forces, who were in turn allowed to take part in drug trafficking networks as a form of payoff. Contrary to official interpretations of twentieth-century Mexico as a time of stability and peace, which Mexican history often favorably compares with the emergence of military dictatorships in South America, Cedillo maintains that pervasive violence and state repression constitute the very heart of Cold War–era Mexico. It was in those years, in the second half of the twentieth century, that the "deep state" emerged and grew, and a new system of power, one in which drug trafficking played a fundamental role, was consolidated. To be clear, this is not the story of a state that was somehow infected or tainted by an evil external force, but the story of a state that became so by suppressing any trace of the bloody secret wars that married counterinsurgency and drug trafficking. When Felipe Calderón declared his war on drugs in 2006, he lifted the veil of the gruesome, inescapable violence that had been integral to the lives of many in the poorer parts of the country. Now it was the urban middle class' turn to experience it. Now we would all be on the front lines. We would face a horror created by a state that had fully submitted to the economic interests of globalization and colonialism; a state that had done nothing more than repeat the famous gesture of Pontius Pilate, the betrayer: that metaphorical handwashing of those unable, or unwilling, to bear responsibility for their actions. The neoliberal Mexican state thus turned its back on its obligations and responsibilities, surrendering before the unrelenting, lethal logic of maximum profit. This came to a head during Carlos Salinas de Gortari's presidency (1988–1994), when fundamental land and labor rights granted by the Mexican Constitution of 1917 were restructured under what is known as the Salinas Reforms. Throughout this book, I call this state, which has rescinded its responsibility for the care of its constituents' bodies, the Visceraless State.[3]

State is a verb, not a noun; state, like capital, is a relationship. In a unilateral move in the beginning of the twenty-first century, the Mexican state, administered by an enthusiastic generation of Ivy League–educated technocrats convinced of the supremacy of profit above life, withdrew protection and care for the bodies of its peoples, thus creating, in Giorgio

Agamben's terms, "the open."[4] Right there, on that atrocious stage, the bodies of all Mexicans were transformed from vulnerable—a regular mode of the human condition—to helpless—an artificial state caused by torture. In its indifference and neglect, in its intricate understanding of the political and even the public, in its indolence, the Visceraless State thus produces the eviscerated body: those chunks of torsos, those legs and feet, that interior that becomes exterior, hanging.

In a lucid essay about what is wrong with the world today, humanist Tony Judt compares the level of aggression and neglect that people suffer at the hands of the totalitarian state to societies where state insufficiencies allow impunity and violence.[5] The latter, without a doubt, is the case in Mexico. A telling clue was revealed in one of former Mexican president Vicente Fox's (2000–2006) on-air interviews. "Why should I care?" he said, directly referring to a dispute involving TV stations, but indirectly betraying his ideas about social well-being and the role of the state in social and cultural matters. "Why should I care?" said the then-president of Mexico in a careless tone, chilling even today. With such a cynical phrase, he solidified the tone of Mexico's particular form of contemporary horrorism.

In close complicity with the members of the executive and judicial branches of the Mexican government, the fierce businessmen of our postmodern, globalized society—the narco—have conspired, with organic if not filial speed, to form a Pontius Pilate state. A product in some cases of the inequalities and hierarchies of an economic system based on dispossession and extraction, the narco has strategically and successfully worked for decades to validate itself as an essential entity in our everyday lives. The corridos and narco novels of this early period often presented a sympathetic portrait of men who grew up in poverty only to become Robin Hood types that provided for their communities when society was not able to or not interested in doing so. Newspaper articles and the media also contributed to a more prominent image of the narco as the B-side of the state. In *Los cárteles no existen* (The cartels do not exist), Oswaldo Zavala argues that cartels were and are so intrinsically enmeshed in the state machinery as to become a part of it.[6] Government corruption along with the narco's signature executions demonstrate what was once easy to deny: drug lords are businessmen prepared to go as far as necessary—which frequently means that space where the human condition ends—in order to ensure and, above all, increase their profits.

Over the last several decades of the twentieth century, we Mexicans have been forced to witness the reduction of the body to its most basic form: as a producer of capital through both the maquilas and other transnational companies. The bare body has emerged, too, when the narco and the state—the narco state—have used the unilateral and spectacular violence of torture against the population. Mouths gaping, hairs standing on end, cold as statues, truly paralyzed, we have done the only thing we could do in the face of such horror: part our lips and mouth wordlessly. As Cavarero recalls, even Primo Levi argued that the most important witnesses, those who have returned alive from an encounter with horror, are usually incapable of articulating their experiences.[7] I insist: This is horror and nothing but horror. This is why it exists. This is its very root. On the other end of the spectrum, however, lies suffering. And where there is suffering, there is voice. Those who suffer have faced horror and come back. The language of pain allows sufferers, those who acknowledge their suffering and share it with others, to articulate an inexpressible experience as an intrinsic criticism against the sources that made it possible in the first place. When everything falls silent, when the gravity of the facts far surpasses our understanding and even our imagination, then there it is—ready, open, stammering, injured, babbling—the language of pain, the pain we share with others.

And this is the importance of suffering, for where suffering lies, so, too, does grieving: the deep sorrow that binds us within emotional communities willing and able to face life anew, even if it means, or especially when it means, radically revising and altering the world we share. There, where suffering lies, so, too, does the political imperative to say, You pain me, I suffer with you, I grieve myself with you. We mourn us. Yours is my story, and my story is ours, because from the start, from the singular—yet generalized—perspective of we who suffer, you are my country, my countries. Hence the aesthetic urgency of expressing, in the most basic and also the most disjointed language possible, This hurts me. Edmond Jabès was right when he critiqued Theodor Adorno's dictum: It isn't that after horror we should not or cannot write poetry. It's that, while we are integral witnesses to horror, we must write poetry differently.[8] Can writing demand the restitution of a Visceral State? Like the Mothers of the Plaza de Mayo, who confronted the atrocities of the military dictatorship in Argentina, and like the Arpillera movement in Chile, which tried to challenge Pinochet's horror, and like the relatives of the disappeared in Mexico, who tread on this land of open graves searching for their loved ones, claiming both justice and restitution? Can writing keep us company—we, the broken ones still alive with rage and hope? I believe writing can, indeed. At the very least, writing should. As demonstrated by the brave journalists who have lent ears to the voices of hundreds of thousands of victims, writing gives us the tools to articulate the mute disarticulation we face on a daily basis. As we write, as we work with language—the humblest and most powerful force available to us—we activate the potency of words, phrases, sentences. Writing as we grieve, grieving as we write: a practice able to create refuge from the open. Writing with others. Grieving like someone who takes refuge from the open. Grieving, which is always a radically different mode of writing.[9]

It is impossible to grieve in the first-person singular. We always grieve for someone and with someone. Grieving connects us in ways that are subtly and candidly material. I am not yet sure which group I should join, where to envision myself, on whose shoulder to cry. I know that pain frequently finds its own allies. A long religious tradition, far from the most rancid institutions of conservative Catholicism, testifies to some of the most politically effective uses of social suffering in our history. Remember, for example, our independence movement, which was led in the early stages, between 1810 and 1815, by the image of the Virgin of Guadalupe—an era when the insurgency was able to gather widespread support. Remember, among so many examples, the Tomochic Rebellion, inspired by Teresa Urrea, la Santa Niña de Cabora, a saintly figure from northern Mexico who voiced the pain and frustration, as well as the hopes, of so many right before the eruption of the Mexican Revolution of 1910. Remember, in short, so much.

On July 16, 1990, Liliana Rivera Garza, my younger sister, was the victim of a femicide. Soon after she was pronounced dead, the Mexico City police had gathered enough evidence to issue a warrant of arrest against an ex-boyfriend who never stopped stalking and threatening her, and who, to this day, has not paid for his crime. My sister, a brilliant architecture student at the UAM Azcapotzalco campus, thus ceased to exist. She was twenty years old. Even

now, thirty years later, the immensity of this fact obliter-
ates me. The war, this variously named war that still tears
us apart, began, for me, on that date. Grieving, too, began its
long, mercurial, transformative work. From utter denial to
unleashed rage, from emotional numbness to bouts of self-
destruction and depression, grieving reshaped me from the
inside out, bringing me together with others. So much has happened since, but it was right after the paralysis of my first contact with horror that I chose language. I wrote before my sister
was mercilessly murdered, but I truly began writing, and writing for her, when my missing her became physically unbear-
able. I did not write to avoid pain, just the opposite. I wrote,
and write, to grieve with others, which is the only secular way I
know to keep her alive. I do not want to avoid suffering. I want
to think through and with pain, and to painfully embrace it, to
give it back its beating heart with which this country—these
countries—still palpitates. When confronted with Medusa's
head, precisely at that moment, because that's when we are
most at risk of becoming stones, right there, say it: Here, you
and me, you and them, we together, we are in pain. We grieve.
Grieving breaks us apart, indeed, and keeps us together.

If the political, as Jacques Rancière argues, "consists in the
changing of places and the counting of bodies,"[10] if the political
is the "activity that breaks with the order of the police by inventing new subjects. Politics invents new forms of collective enun-
ciation; it re-frames the given by inventing new ways of making
sense of the sensible,"[11] then this painful book, these sorrowful
essays, are more than a mere attempt to empathize with the
victims. They are, if they are anything, an exercise in dissensus
that has to be able to bring back into play, and in another way,
"what can be perceived, thought and done."[12] These texts, I
mean to say, are political. They do not beg for commiseration;

they are not subject to the market of pity. They do not try to take away or give space to the multiple voices that already exist. Quite the contrary. More so, in an effort to oppose a discourse of war that gives preference to state violence and the violence of the businessmen of the globalized world, these dispatches implicate pain, the suffering of the eviscerated body, in order to participate in the reconfiguration of "what can be seen, what can be said and what can be thought and, consequently, a new landscape of the possible."[13]

One day, on a cloudy March afternoon to be more exact, I was in a classroom lined with long, rectangular windows in an old colonial building in the heart of Mexico City. Through one of those windows, in the most surprising manner, someone entered. It was a young man. He said he'd come from Oaxaca and that he wanted to meet me. I believe he sat in on the session in which we discussed the methods of documentary poetry, the writing practice that incorporates and subverts, that embraces and tests the public language of the dispossessed and the suffering. The participants of that workshop put together a blog consisting of texts that were made up of the words from the mothers and fathers of the forty-nine children massacred in the ABC Day Care Center Fire in Hermosillo, Sonora, in 2009. Later, that same young man who came in through the window as if it were a door asked me for something impossible, which is the only thing worth asking for. Saúl Hernández, that's his name, asked me to articulate in a book my ideas about the current situation in Mexico. He wasn't interested in the historian's or the writer's point of view or version of events. Saúl wanted the words of the dweller of this world who was simultaneously—who cannot cease being—a historian and a writer and a mother and a daughter and a sister. A grieving sister. It only took me a few minutes to understand that this, and nothing else, would be my next book. I quickly understood that this book, which would come as a result of a reader's invitation, would be a truly collaborative work, something that came over me as much as through me. The impossible works like this sometimes. I gathered articles I had written and published as well as texts that had not yet seen the light of day. I included poems and crónicas and personal essays. Essays written directly in English also found their place in these pages. I did not respect a chronological order but carefully organized the sequence in which each text would appear. The internal dialogue. The ceaseless drifting. I was convinced that the book should be a tactile experience, as Mark Rothko wanted from all artistic practices; I wanted the air to get in it. The air of the present. In reality, this doesn't end until it ends.

Confronting Medusa, who is also a head separated from a body; confronting Medusa, who is also a decapitated woman, I avoid the mirror, which is another way of avoiding being turned into stone, and I accept the consequences, all human and all final, of words. These are my sentences.

The Sufferers

I

The Claimant

Excuse me, Señor Presidente, for not extending
my hand
you are not my friend. I
cannot welcome you
You are not welcome
no one is.

*Luz María Dávila, Villas de Salvárcar, mother of Marcos and
José Luis Piña Dávila, nineteen and seventeen years old.*

It isn't fair
my little boys were at a party
and they were killed.

*Massacre of Saturday, January 30, in Ciudad Juárez, Chihuahua,
fifteen deaths.*

Because here
in Ciudad Juárez, put yourself in my place

Villas de Salvárcar, my back, my fulminous paradox

for two years they have been committing murders
they are committing many things

to commit is a shining verb, a radiant vertigo, a lethargic
tremor

they are committing many things and no one does
anything.
And I only want there to be
justice, and not only for my two boys

the dead distressed, the fulminous massacred, the shining lost
ones

but for everyone. Justice.

To confront, spit out, claim, accuse, demand, call for, require,
defend

Don't tell me "of course," do something!
If your child had been killed
you would leave no stone unturned looking for the
murderer

under the rocks, under rocks, under

but because I don't have the resources

alms for the birds, my bones
my flesh
from your flesh my flesh

put yourself in my place, put yourself
my shoes, my nails, my stellar shiver

**I can't look for them because I don't have
resources, I have
the death of my two sons**

Byagtor: burial in open sky that literally means "give alms to
the birds."

I have my back. My tear. My hammer.
I don't have justice. Put yourself
in their place: Villas de Salvárcar, there
where they killed my two sons.

You are not my friend, this
is the hand I do not extend to you, put yourself
Señor Presidente
in your place, I give you
my back

my thirst, I give you, my unknown shiver, my distressed
tenderness, my shining birds, my dead

*And the short woman, with the blue sweater, left the room wiping
away her tears.*[1]

II

The Visceraless State

On November 29, 1939, a young patient writing from "Ward 26 M.4 bis, Upstairs" sent a letter to Rodolfo Faguarda, then governor of the North Territory of Baja California, whose offices were located in the palacio de gobierno of Mexicali, Baja California. With beautiful handwriting, respecting the invisible lines on the page, Señorita, that's how she signed her name, described in detail the situation of her health, which was, at the same time, the situation of her body. The situation of her insides.

In virtue of having waited for more than a year in repose in this hospital waiting for a radical cure and not being able to get it, Dr. Chief of This Ward has suggested I write to you, Mr. Governor, to inform you that it is necessary that I return to Baja California and that my illness is not ceding but neither is it advancing, that my sputum analyses are always negative and that my blood and basal metabolic analyses are also negative. Furthermore, the climate here has left me with a cold and an uncontrollable cough that tends to be asthmatic but that, in spite of everything, does not pose the risk of infection. In regard to my stomach, it's chronic constipation. The white blotches are also chronic. Not able to do anything on my part, I ask you, urgently, to intervene on my behalf.

The public administrator signed the acknowledgment of receipt of this letter on November 30 of the same year, archiving it with the number 14508 in the record 852/641.1/856. In pencil, in the margins of the original letter, an anonymous hand wrote the next day:

Transcribe it to C[itizen] Secretary of Public Assistance, requesting that he kindly arrange to attend to this Govt. report concerning the present state of the ill woman as well as the necessity there may be for her to leave the hospital where she is. Copy the interested party.

A few months later, on February 17, 1940, the public administrator transcribed a letter sent to C[itizen] General Secretary of the North Territory Government in which the state of the young patient's health is detailed. Again, written observations of her body abound: "spasmodic cough, dyspnea on exertion, chronic constipation."

The señorita never backed down in her efforts. Toward the end of December, for example, she informed the governor of the state of her teeth: "They are all decayed and four molars need to be pulled." In other letters, some from the Zoquiapan sanatorium, she also elaborated on the cold or bronchitis that had caused her to "stay in bed for weeks." The first thing that caught my attention was a letter from July 16, 1941, in which our Señorita Signatory informed the governor that they would soon operate on her in the general hospital.

They are going to operate on me, that is, they are going to remove four ribs. They will probably do it soon. As I will not be able to inform you of the result later, I urgently beg you, Mr. Governor, to do me the favor of informing the capital's public assistance program of the state of my health. God willing, I stay alive and healthy. I do not want them to operate on me. I also would prefer they do not autopsy my body after death. I ask you, Mr. Governor, to intervene on my behalf with your valuable influence so that they give me a grave in some cemetery and that my body not be reduced to ashes.

The correspondence between Señorita Signatory and the various state agencies on both the local and federal level continues beyond what's excerpted above and certainly requires a more careful analysis. But I stopped here, where the shock began and where my interest was piqued, because it was right here that, with justified fear and perhaps unjustified trust, the issue of the fate of her body repeatedly appears. The final resting place of her organs. For this woman without a family to turn to, her ultimate fate was not a minor nor a merely personal question in a strict sense—her organs were a question of the state.

If social historians are to be believed, much of what was written about and by the Mexican state at the end of the nineteenth century was done using the language of medicine. Essentially performing the work of urban planners or professional legislators, medical professionals not only examined the social body but also ushered citizens' bodies toward the stretcher of the state, figuratively as much as literally. Naming the body—above all, naming the body's interior, its organs—was one of the first steps recounted in the triumphant histories of the professionalization of medicine and some of its branches (psychiatry among them, but also gynecology). The system of public hospitals that formed an important part of the government's structure following the 1910 Mexican Revolution did nothing but increase the bodily relationship between the state and its citizens. The letters from Señorita Signatory clearly communicate that this relationship was visceral for both parties—state and citizen—and they communicate with certainty—whether real or fictitious, whether in actuality or grasped at—that the care and fate of her body was, effectively, a question of the state.

I think about the numerous letters that Señorita Signatory sent to the governor, about the numerous transcribed acknowledgments of receipt and responses that were issued from the office of that governor, while I look at a photograph of a woman's body suspended, hanged, from a pedestrian bridge in Monterrey, Nuevo León. It is the last day of 2010, and there is something, in addition to the woman's neck, definitively broken in the image. It has been a long time since the postrevolutionary governments gave way to the welfare state and, in turn, to the neoliberal state. How long ago was it that Vicente Fox—famously or infamously, depending on the political alliances of the person remembering—said: Why should I care?

In the terrible reality summed up in that question lies part of the explanation of the growing violence that is practiced in Mexico today by and against the body. When the neoliberal state put aside its responsibility for the bodies of its citizens, when it stopped "intervening on their behalf," the well-being of its communities, the relationship that had been established with and from the people at the beginning of the twentieth century, slowly but inevitably began to dissolve. The impunity of an inefficient and corrupt justice system has only confirmed the fundamental neglect and the brutal indifference of a state that only conceives of itself as an administrative system, not as a governmental relationship. This, then, is my hypothesis: the neoliberal state, until now dominated by conservative Panista governments (though by no means limited to that party tendency), has not established bad-faith relationships with its citizens but something even worse and more chilling. The neoliberal state has established visceraless relationships with its citizens. Relationships without hearts or bones or innards. Disemboweled relationships. The misnamed war on drugs has certainly emphasized the spectacle of disemboweled bodies in cities as well as in the countryside, but otherwise it has done nothing but follow the cynical Foxian question to its logical end: If you don't care, then I care even less. And as proof, there is the body of a woman hanging from a pedestrian bridge, which spans from the first to the second decade of the twenty-first century.

There is no doubt that the real, or in any case the most literal, heirs of the seventy years of rule by the Partido Revolucionario Institucional (PRI) in the twentieth century have been the drug cartels. Usurping protest language (from the sixties' mantas, or banners, to their debatable identification with the most vulnerable strata of society) and establishing patronage relationships with certain well-chosen communities (the exchange of certain urban improvements for social support, for example), those successful businessmen of the globalized world participate in an interpretation of capitalism as a defleshed capitalism. If the head of the executive branch of the government itself questioned why he should care, then the narco-businessmen care even less. And on this very point, the neoliberal state and the narco couldn't agree more. If it is necessary to choose between profits and the body, the final decision will always be for profit. Confirming the theses that Viviane Forrester puts forth in *The Economic Horror*, it is clear that, for the narco as much as for the neoliberal state, work—and the human body that carries out that work in the deepest sense of the term, in the sense of work as a process of transforming the world and making reality subjective—is no longer essential for the operation of capitalism nor for the survival of the planet.[1] While those in power continue asking "why should I care," they let those who work keep tearing each other apart. The bodies.

I reread the letters that Señorita Signatory sent, in the middle of another century, from various public hospitals to the governor of a remote zone of Mexico. I reread how the woman describes her pain, expressing it without affected modesty and with great care for the names of her body's organs. Her lungs. Her teeth. Her bones. I reread the way she refuses to be converted to ashes, and I stop again, surprised. Only someone who lives in a world, now, where the body has finally been superseded by profit could sigh like this at the words for bodily organs. Only someone who has already seen too much of our insides on the street—heads, fingers, ears, blood—could read this letter from the public archive as a love letter between the state and citizen. Only someone who has begun the second decade of the twenty-first century with the almost routine image of a body hanging, like a pendulum, from a pedestrian bridge, could think that these documents are, really, evidence of something visceral.

To be clear, nostalgia does not compel me. I am not writing about these letters, about this woman's organs, or the shocking contrast between them and our current Visceraless State, to invoke a return to some mythical past where things were somehow better or less cruel. At least before we didn't see heads rolling on the ground! In the past, photographers saved the images of the hanged bodies for the pages of the nota roja and it did not occur to anyone to put them in the society pages! I am aware, as one should be, that the relations established by the Mexican state at the beginning of the postrevolutionary phase, which I have chosen to call visceral, soon gave rise to forms of social co-optation and subordination that in many ways paved the way for the emergence of the neoliberal state, the one that no longer took on, "on their behalf," the care of the body and, consequently, of the community. I am aware. What I do want to write today—at the very beginning of 2011, when a "fourteen-year-old girl was found in chaparrals in the municipality of Zitlala," according to *El Universal*, or when @menosdias, the death counter, reported in a tweet: "Coyuca de Catalán Guerrero Dec. 31. 4 men died during the final minutes of the night while they attended a party in the fields," or when the newspapers discuss with ease the more than thirty thousand deaths the misnamed war on drugs has cost us— is that I fear that no change of government, no reform in the justice system, will be able to transform this spectacle of violence until the state is prepared to accept the responsibility established in the Constitution of 1917. After all, we are in an embodied relationship. To the neoliberal governments' cynical disregard for the body, we have to respond with the pained voices of today: yes, you should care, you above all, certainly, but we all should. We ought to. Our bodies are under our care. Our organs are materials for which we are responsible. The dead are mine and they are yours. The responsibility of the representative of the executive power is, indeed, to execute— but *execute* comes from the Latin *exsecutus*, past participle of *exsequi*, which means to consummate, to fulfill. *Execute* does not mean to kill.

I do not know if the body of this woman, the one who wrote letters to her governor, was buried or reduced to ashes against her will. I am continuously surprised, as a citizen of a visceraless state, that long correspondence between patient-citizens and government agencies that, like it or not, believing it to be their duty or not, dealt with their petitions and claims. Those responses that declared, in their own way: I do care. All for a body. All for the still-existent, though admittedly imperfect, relationship between the body and the state. All for one's insides. It is the forgetting of the body, the erasure of the body, in both political and personal terms, that opens the door to violence. Those who are believed to no longer be human will be the ones to walk through it.

III

War and Imagination

In the 2006 novel *The Inheritance of Loss* by Kiran Desai—a writer born in India with residency in the United States and England—Gyan, a young and impoverished mathematics tutor, joins, almost by accident, the Gorkha Liberation Army. Like many inhabitants of Nepal, Gyan resents British as much as Indian colonialism, but on the afternoon that he marches in a protest, his actions have more to do with the fact that he knows many of the members—old college classmates—than with his distinctly political convictions. As he moves with them through the streets of Kalimpong, raising his voice along with the others, first the giddy sensation of making history arises, and then, almost immediately, comes the sensation of *playing at* making history. The division breaks him down. Suddenly, looking at himself from the outside, he cannot help but notice the everyday elements of those streets with a melancholy that, in many ways, seems like affection: the traffic, the local shops (the deaf tailors, the blacksmiths, the homeopathic pharmacy), the crazy woman that runs by. "Then, looking at the hills, he fell out of the experience again. How can the ordinary be changed?" he wonders.[1] While he remembers how

Indian settlers came together to demand the eviction of the British presence in the peninsula, recalling the glory and risk that shaped the latent marrow of liberated India, Gyan reflects, "If a nation had such a climax in its history, its heart, would it not hunger for it again?"[2]

I often consider similar questions, especially now in 2009 as we approach the close of another of the hundred-year cycles that marks the emergence of the Independence movement and revolution in Mexico, each of which began, at least formally, on the tenth year of each new century. 1810. 1910. I consider these questions ahistorically, then, in a year that has begun with a wave of violence that urban generations born toward the end of the twentieth century have only heard about in stories from grandparents or in certain novels or history books or even in movies. History, everything seems to indicate, is already regressing in its dream of progress and globalization. Awake, history hungrily moves through the city streets or countryside. Sleepless jaws. History reminds us, as always, that we are mortal. That there are things left unresolved.

In *Los grandes problemas nacionales* (The great national problems),[3] the detailed analysis of Mexican history published in 1909, Andrés Molina Enríquez argues that early twentieth-century Mexico's great problem was not, as Francisco I. Madero claims in his book *The Presidential Succession of 1910*,[4] democracy, or more precisely, the lack of democracy, but land. In his opinion, based on long-term historical data, Mexico's problem was not merely political but profoundly material: ownership of the land. With a higher concentration of land owned, greater inequality. With a higher concentration of wealth in the hands of a few, greater exploitation of labor. With greater exploitation of labor, greater possibilities of popular violence. As opposed to what Molina Enríquez, son of a norteño landowner and educated in Paris, believed, by not resolving it, this inequality would continue to pull the country into the cycle of ancestral violence. The problem will not be resolved, then, in the voting urns, but in the context in which those urns were produced.

We must remember that, according to some historians, the conquest of Mexico actually coincided with a wave of popular uprisings against Aztec power, which was growing increasingly distant from its peoples. If the Indigenous chronicles of the period are trustworthy, we must remember that the Spaniards were not the only ones to call Moctezuma "dog," and that his own people were the ones to throw the rocks that would finish him. We must also remember that of all the mobilizations that resulted in independence throughout Latin America, only the Mexican one was a true attempt at structural revolution—at least between 1810 and 1815, under the leadership of Hidalgo and Morelos. It is enough to read José María Morelos Pavón's marvelous document *Los sentimientos de la nación* (The feelings of the nation)—we are a nation into whose founding letters slip, effectively, the word *feeling*—to recognize what resides in the very marrow of this country: equality between races, distribution of the land, devotion to the Virgin of Guadalupe. And we must remember that, as Molina Enríquez argues in his thick treatise, even when Madero became president of Mexico, the lack of popular support, marked by the distance between him and what peasant-leader Zapata established in the Plan of Ayala, directly caused—without a mediating metaphor—his death.

What did it feel like to live in those times? How is a revolution forged from daily life? In the words of Gyan, Kiran Desai's character, "How can the ordinary be changed?" According to those who adhere to the "teoría de la bola," or "ball theory," all social mobilizations may be explained by the snowball effect—a possibly "natural" process that is, in any case, irrational, especially affecting the working classes of a country. Someone begins by knowing little or very little, and others, knowing even less, follow them. Why? Just to follow. To follow the ball. Some historians have worked more or less explicitly with this kind of notion. And the same idea is present in *The Underdogs*, the famous novel by Mariano Azuela, in which a middle-class, urban, civilized doctor develops a disgust for the pointless ferocity of the peasants and soldaderas he lives with during the revolutionary years.[5] Not all visions of the revolution, however, are so classist (and racist and chauvinist). There are also those who have argued that structural disparities—economic, political, or cultural—are what pulse at the heart of an uprising. This, of course, and hope. Who, not believing there is something better ahead, in that other place that is not yet here, could leave their house one morning and take up arms in protest? Who, not believing there is something to be gained, because everything is lost in what is, could wield a weapon that will end a life that represents an entire system of death?

From all the descriptions of the period, I prefer Nellie Campobello's *Cartucho*, an unclassifiable book in which the eyes of a girl allow us to see not only what was happening in northern Mexico at the beginning of the twentieth century but also what is still happening in the country one hundred years later, at the beginning of the twenty-first century.[6] *My dead men. The toys of my childhood. My decapitated bodies.* Without sentimentalisms, with an almost exasperating austerity, the girl registers daily violence in a way that neither novelists from the period nor historians of another have been able to emulate. Although they all speak of the violence with either a greater or lesser level of fascination, only the girl sees it. There is a naturalness with which it emerges on the streets (*my childhood toys*), a bloody, everydayness of its occurrence. Does the early twenty-first-century novelist already think of the "decapitated bodies" that appear on the streets and on the television and in the press as her childhood toys? Does she see them now with the same detachment, the same strength that Campobello assigns to her young female character? Has that young girl already experienced fear? Does she already know that she should not leave her parents' side in the supermarket for fear of being kidnapped, or has she already attended the funeral where she said goodbye to her father or mother or friend? Does this girl already know that she cannot go out in the evening or at night because the city, that jumble of streets, does not belong to her nor to those who are like her, extirpated thus of their citizenship? Has this future novelist already felt the wild pounding of her heart when the military command vertiginously passes by, and then the siren of the ambulance and then the silence that follows, burying everything in the darkest night? Does this novelist already know that the most lethal writing about the Mexico she was born into is not found in books but on the mantas containing threats and boasts that appear up and down the country, hung by the cartels in every city, from the most remote to the most populated?

In *The Cultural Politics of Emotion*, Sara Ahmed argues that politicians frequently turn to fear as an emotion able to galvanize their own agendas.[7] Malleable, fear alerts the body to danger, indeed, but if felt for a long time, it also numbs, paralyzes. A society that is afraid is a society that looks down. Those who are afraid fail to act. Imprisoned by fear, the frightened hear noises that, at night, infuriatingly stretch until dawn, and, by day, fall in step with them. Those who are afraid waste most of their energy bracing themselves for blows that are not, for them, imaginary. Mentally crouching, they await the crucial moment—the decision that, even if trivial, or perhaps because it is trivial, will trigger the end of their inner world. Few emotions make us so aware of the bloody repercussions of every tiny act like fear does. Simply standing on a corner, turning your head, knowing a certain person, having met at a party— all of this can become, with the passage of time, the cause of that shooting, that kidnapping, that rape. In expansion, blown out of proportion, no decision in your daily life escapes paranoia. Fear isolates. Fear teaches us to mistrust. Fear drives us crazy. With hands in pockets and head bent forward, those who are afraid are thus transformed into the ultimate tool of the status quo.

Perhaps the most explicit contemporary example of the political usage of fear was former president George W. Bush's unashamed manipulation of September 11, 2001. Exhorting a holy war against Islam and promoting the hatred that cultivated the aggression itself in the first place, Bush plunged the United States into a panic-induced stupor that deactivated the creative energy—*politically* creative energy—of its inhabitants. Congregated under the flag of a patriotism of lowered heads and closed eyes, the people of the United States got used to being searched in airports, to being registered in their private residences. Dissidence, as is well known, was silenced under the pretext of betrayal. Susan Sontag experienced this firsthand when she dared to question the set of criteria Bush appealed to in the aftermath of 9/11, and that he obtained widespread support for.[8] Declaring a war—against Islam or against drug trafficking—always has consequences. All of them disastrous. Predicated on fear and on multiplying that fear, the wars that those in power invite us to participate in are the best part of a bad deal. In this case, though it appears to be the opposite, we have nothing to gain. There, under the guise of winning (security, stability, protection), we are, in reality, losing. The soldier who dies in service knows it and the one who is grazed by a bullet meant for someone else knows it; the woman arrested for nothing more than having walked on the street knows it and the driver searched ad nauseam at the border knows it; and those who attend the funerals know it, and the future writer who has already learned to look knows it. Seeing *this*.

It was the Italian Alessandro Baricco who, in the introduction for his contemporary reimagining of *The Iliad*, called on us to think about alternatives to war.[9] It has always existed, he alleges. It is in the bones of the most diverse civilizations: the adrenaline of war, the excitement of war, the hypnotic song of war. Only when societies can invent something more exciting, riskier, more adventurous, more revolutionary, will we be able to say, truthfully, that we are against war. A form of radical pacifism. A tenacious provocation, certainly.

Following Andrés Molina Enríquez, that positivist from the beginning of the twentieth century, I repeat now what was already known then: only when the problem of social inequality is properly addressed can we truly address the heart of that nation (with its feelings) called Mexico. Following Alessandro Baricco, I repeat: if we want to go beyond a war based on fear, a war whose goal is to produce more fear, we should imagine something more stimulating, more enraged; something with more adrenaline. With the situationists of some fifty years ago, I repeat that our task is not to declare war (or to respond to a declaration of war) but to produce from below and as a community a dynamic and creative, emotional and fulfilling, everyday life. And it is right there that, humbly and even discreetly, words enter: the written words—the books from which they jump into view, and from there, into the whole body and imagination. Those who imagine can always imagine that *this*, whatever *this* is, can be different. This is the critical power of imagination. Those who can imagine, by walking down the streets of Ciudad Juárez, that they are, effectively, walking down the streets of Baghdad, can also question the naturalness with which the militarization of cities tends to be introduced. Those who imagine know, and they know from within, that nothing is natural. Nothing is inevitable. I bet that girl, the future novelist of the twenty-first century, knows it too.

IV

On *Diary of Pain* by María Luisa Puga

Several years ago, when I was teaching at San Diego State University, I organized the seminar Social Suffering and Redemption in Historical Perspectives—a class for graduate students in which we explored some of the ways that different societies have produced and experienced the materiality and symbolism of pain. We began by reading Elaine Scarry's magnificent book *The Body in Pain*, a careful revision of documents produced around political torture. We continued with *The Culture of Pain* by David B. Morris, with its particularly interesting interpretations of pain from popular culture. At the end of the first session, we talked about *Social Suffering*, a volume edited by Arthur Kleinman, Veena Das, and Margaret Lock, which is, without a doubt, one of the books that has contributed to the official onset of the thus-named studies on human suffering. With the help of these three books, we were able to establish the central questions that, with each new reading, we would end up hopelessly returning to throughout the semester: If pain occurs beyond language, as Scarry argues, then what does it silence? If painful experiences change from one society to the next and from one historical period to another, what is essential in pain, if anything? In what ways does pain produce the body and not vice versa? And if it is necessary to discuss that which cannot be discussed, how can we think through pain without making it a commodity or a formula of exchange? Each and every one of these questions, and many more that I have forgotten, are sharply, searingly present in María Luisa Puga's 2004 memoir *Diario del dolor* (Diary of pain), which is, regrettably, not yet translated into English.[1] It is a book that not only expresses her everyday relationship with chronic rheumatoid arthritis but also with writing. An affliction. Two.

Divided into one hundred short, fragmented, fragile-as-bone entries, the book neither advances nor recedes but finds itself suspended in that emptiness that the author compares to "having remained in anesthesia."[2] Without sentimentalisms, avoiding, as much as possible, a nostalgic golden age in which her pain did not yet have a name, and also skipping the teleological visitation of its origin, what María Luisa Puga achieves in this text is an exquisite cruelty: not only does she make pain speak but, a writer through and through, she speaks with it. She forces pain to pay attention, and in the end, from within her own writing, she incites it to fall in love with itself with the same "narcissistic rejoicing" of the aging.[3] Her *Diario del dolor* is that wordless conversation, that dialogue held in silent cries, this you-to-you that the person in pain establishes, actively and without any compassion, with her other Other, her simile, her internal shadow. Her pain. Because the truth is that, since it appeared, since it made itself known, that is to say, since the very beginning of her diary, just as it is noted there, the author was never again alone.

More than an illness: a romance. Or, even better: an illness and a romance. A romance that is all illness. In these pages, the pain will come to substitute the novel—because the novel is carried, Puga is right, like an aureole in and outside her head—and her friends and her body itself, and, eventually, reality. Pain is able to overwhelm everything except for writing. Pain recedes, falters, tiptoes, when writing begins. Turned into that third apocalyptic point of view that sees and registers, writing stabilizes the angle from which Puga speaks to her pain. "It looks at me insistently," the author writes, "saying to me: I recognize you perfectly; you don't recognize me perfectly yet, but you will—I will tire otherwise. I accept you without greater resistance, but I won't do anything. I let myself be."[4] Pain, as the author carefully notes later, shows itself to be "skeptical before the notebook."[5] And, at least for those moments vis-à-vis the manuscript, the two turn their backs on each other. She would go as far as to affirm that writing allows them both—pain and herself—to rest.

In the sections in which pain pushes her to suspend her judgment, María Luisa Puga describes how she makes the bed or how she moves throughout the house in a chair that has wheels but that is not a wheelchair. All of this without a trace of self-pity. All of this with an austere sense of modesty. These are the tentative steps of someone entering a private world. And what to say about the way in which chairs hurt her? How to even approximate the burning caused by a wrinkle in her sheets? How to imagine the cane that picks up her diabolical shampoo cap? How to not sit with the book in your hands, your gaze suspended on some other emptiness that hangs from another loose thread, when Puga describes the MAN (the capitalization is hers) that accompanies her and eases her life with the following words: "I feel very good in the truck, just that sometimes I look at him out of the corner of my eye and I know that something happened to him: an embolism that paralyzed the right side of his body, or, that is to say, me."[6]

To accept or submit to the dictates of pain is, just as Judith Butler writes about mourning, to accept that everything will change.[7] This is the diary of that kind of surrender. Here the author speaks to pain—now with rage or resignation, now with a desire to never see it again or with a pining for it when it seems to leave, now in the colloquialism of a joke or an unpleasant user's manual—like the Other for whom the door is, finally, open. This is your house. This is their house. This is, by grace of the word, our house too. The house of the most arduous transformation. The house where the body falls.

V

Tragic Agency

It is difficult to write about pain. The risks involved in trying
to grasp its social contexts and embody its human cracks and
nooks and crannies, as Susan Sontag recalls in *Regarding the
Pain of Others*, range from easy sensationalism to exhausting
sentimentality—forms of interpretation that, instead of pro-
voking an implied response or active empathy, instead transform any old scene of suffering into a stereotype, or worse,
keep it at a stony distance.[1] The difficulty of writing about
pain comes from our interpretations that regularly yield to
the way things are or that reproduce pain in all its rawness or
impotency or verticality. Studies pushing back against these
kinds of approaches emerged in the last quarter of the twentieth century, privileging the perspectives of the weakest and,
when relevant, of the victims. In their eagerness to offer the
other version, the alternative perspective, the gaze that moves
from the bottom up, many of these analyses transformed
the sufferer into a hero, even in spite of themselves. Thus, by
emphasizing social agency—the people's capacity to produce their own story through strategies involving resistance,

adaptation, or negotiation—these studies became, whether they meant to or not, narratives of heroism: stories that were quite linear and positive in which the agent not only appears as proactive but is also oriented toward concrete—if not felicitous—results. But what do you do with someone who tries but is not successful and, not having succeeded, then desists? Where do you place the person who, devastated by suffering, only manages to articulate it and, even then, falteringly? The study of social suffering, an interdisciplinary field that became increasingly prominent toward the end of the twentieth century, has tried, in fact, to find answers to these kinds of questions. Among other things, these inquiries have made me think about another kind of agency. Without being passive—an act is always an act, after all—this agent clamors for an alternative denomination: tragic.

A term that necessarily takes us back to Aristotle's *Poetics* and commonly signifies fatalism (for in a tragedy, the hero is destroyed), *tragedy* stages, as John Drakakis and Naomi Conn Liebler put it, the "relationship between suffering and joy in a universe which is often perceived as at best inimical, or at worst radical in its hostility to human life."[2] Whether celebrated as a Dionysian delight in Nietzschean style, or lamented as a world that is opposed to the will of humanity, tragedy includes the important concept of the purgation "of pity and fear," in Aristotelian terms[3]; the process through which human limitations are recognized and accepted. Yet, as Karl Jaspers has argued, tragedy works when it reveals "some particular truth in every agent and at the same time the limitations of this truth, and so to reveal the injustice in everything."[4] This revelatory power has led Raymond Williams, with Bertold Brecht in mind, to perceive tragedy through the lens of suffering and affirmation:

"We have to see not only that suffering is avoidable but that it is not avoided. And not only that suffering breaks us, but that it need not break us. . . . Against the fear of a general death, and against the loss of connection, a sense of life is affirmed, learned as closely in suffering as ever in joy."[5] That is to say, these tragic elements—with their emphasis on suffering and on the limits of human experience that underscore the encounter of opposing forces capable of altering the hierarchies that keep them in their place—have proven particularly useful for social analyses of revolutions.

In modern Mexico, where postrevolutionary generations have turned the 1910 Revolution into an official and foundational epic more or less successfully, little serious attention has been paid to its tragic origins and its tragic subjects. The painful narratives, in which, as in tragedy, the "detail of suffering is insistent, whether as violence or as the reshaping of lives by a new power in the state,"[6] provide the reader with this opportunity. As scholars in the emerging and interdisciplinary field of social suffering have pointed out, suffering is an action, a social and cultural experience that engages the most ominous aspects of modernization and globalization. By considering that historically shaped local forms of suffering merit serious attention, these scholars avoid representing sufferers as inadequate, passive, or fatalist victims. Thus, instead of privileging the "devastating injuries that social force can inflict on the human experience,"[7] more recent studies emphasize the distinct ways in which sufferers identify, bear, and expose the roots of their misfortune.

My understanding of tragic agency, more of an intimation than a concept in and of itself, seeks to discern that which seems to make sense in many narrations of afflictions in the psychiatric hospital: that suffering destroys but it also confers dignity, a higher moral status, to the one that suffers. As Jorge Luis Borges once said, "Men have sought kinship with the defeated Trojans, and not with the victorious Greeks. This is perhaps because there is a dignity in defeat that hardly belongs to victory."[8]

VI

I Won't Let Anyone Say
Those Are the Best Years of Your Life

"I was twenty," French writer Paul Nizan once wrote. Then he added, conspicuously: "I won't let anyone say those are the best years of your life."[1] Teenagers growing up in late twentieth-century Ciudad Juárez could have easily said the same thing. A nameless war, a war allegedly against drugs, broke out, spreading unspeakable acts of violence throughout every city street and the adjacent dunes of the border desert. The war, too, overtook public space, dictating new rules of conviviality, and it ultimately reached the innermost confines of people's homes, where it wreaked havoc and silent scenes of horror. As with other border cities, a black legend of crime and licentiousness has overshadowed Ciudad Juárez since the late nineteenth century, when the proliferation of red-light districts, with its assorted components of prostitution and gambling, facilitated the wide distribution of drugs. Violence was not alien to this border city back then, but the eruption of the US-backed wars on drugs from the early 1970s, all the way through President Felipe Calderón's declaration of war at the beginning of his term in 2007, dramatically transformed the scope and the nature of such violence. Cartels viciously fought for territories they called plazas and the federal government, in alliance with drug lords, neglected to protect the civil population, rendering them helpless before an enemy with the insidious capacity to entice friends and neighbors into its ranks.

While misnamed or unnamed, the mayhem that took over Ciudad Juárez, and eventually a good portion of Mexico, displayed all the rituals associated with war: an official declaration by a head of state, a clear identification of an enemy, the mobilization of armies throughout the territory, and the seizing of enemies and compromising goods. Civil casualties grew exponentially: kidnappings, extortions, and murders as public spectacle became regular headlines in the daily news. Growing militarization was remarkably noticeable in border cities, such as Ciudad Juárez, where the uniforms of both the national army and the federal police were flaunted in the urban landscape. At the same time, the femicide machine continued churning out bodies of poor women working at foreign-owned assembly plants. War altered the way Ciudad Juárez lived and dreamed; the way men and women dwelled, or not, in public spaces; the way young kids made friends and organized parties. As in *Bicycles Are for the Summer*, a play by Fernando Fernán Gómez and a movie directed by Jaime Chávarri, both released in 1984, in which the Spanish Civil War interrupts the adolescence of a group of friends, forcing them to go directly from childhood into adulthood, the kids of Ciudad Juárez were not able to ride their metaphorical bikes over the summer of their lives. Nizan was right: it was by no means a beautiful age.

How did young kids live through this war on the Mexican people, unleashed by the combined interests of drug cartels, the Mexican federal government, and its foreign allies? What did they witness and how did they react? How did they manage to protect themselves? Did they imagine a future for themselves or for their cities, their homes? The testimonies contained in *Estos últimos años en Ciudad Juárez* (These recent years in Ciudad Juárez),[2] a slim book published in 2020 by human rights organization ICIDHAC, Brown Buffalo Press, and Juárez Dialoga, allows us to engage with the answers to these and other crucial questions.

No one survives a war unscathed. Just as rivers feed nearby land by virtue of their mere existence, wounds run deep and pain seeps through every inch of the body. No action, no word, no gesture is unconnected to war. Similarly, actions and words and gestures remain linked to a growing alertness, a critical consciousness, about the sources of tragedy and loss. There are laments in the book, but they are never disassociated from the rage and indignation against both a Visceraless State and the profit-making cartels. Wounded and on their toes at the same time, the people who remember their youth in a war-ravaged Ciudad Juárez, while still, in many cases, confronting the damage brought upon them by forces larger than their own, speak directly and to the point: We were robbed, many testify. They robbed us of our youth, indeed, but more importantly, they robbed us of our future. Participating in this multivocal collection of testimonies may be a first step in regaining control over that long-lost future, which is now our very own present, and along the way the story of those years, the marrow of their life stories, will be remembered. Those years may not have been beautiful, but they were theirs after all.

Many of the twelve authors featured in this collection acknowledge the Salvárcar massacre of January 31, 2010, as a turning point. María Luz Dávila lost her only two sons that night. "Seven vehicles, twenty hitmen, sixteen killed, twelve wounded, all between fifteen and twenty years of age," summarizes Cesar Graciano in "Likely Words." A flash of lightning for an entire generation. The sudden realization that age was not going to spare them from mounting violence. If they had been prone to complain about overprotective mothers, about endless afternoons spent in lonely rooms playing video games, about permissions never granted to attend parties or hang out with friends, now they knew. Or else, they pictured it. José Manuel Bonilla in "Animal Cruelty," and Fabiola Román in "Dream and Fiction," do not sugarcoat it: it was confinement, plain and simple. Bedrooms became cages they could seldom escape. Meanwhile, reality lingered there, out there, alluring and dangerous, something barely graspable, well beyond the window bars. Public space was similarly out of bounds for them. No riding bikes, no going to school on their own, no playing soccer on the street, no movie theaters. Above all, they were not to answer to strangers. In sum: no trust. Friends could have turned out not to be friends. And enemies, larger and more powerful than imagined. The sensation shared by an entire generation: being surrounded by foes in camouflage. "It was not the best time to be sixteen," writes Miguel Silerio in "Untitled."

Confinement and mistrust constituted the basic ground for loss. The actual loss of friends directly killed by the Mexican Army or by the cartel's hitmen; or the less quantifiable, but equally certain, loss of time never shared with others. The loss of affection. Solidarity. Connection. The loss of an age. "And my time, who will reimburse my time?" wonders Graciel S. C. at the start of "A Portrait in Three Subordinations." In "Interior Landscapes," Omar Baca refers not only to present-time snatched out of his hands and consciousness by both the state and the mafia, and ultimately by naked capitalism, but also to future-time. Unsure about what a new day might bring, followed by shootings wherever he went, he soon learned to be cautious about longing. About five years from now. About things to come. Marco Antonio López Romero concurs in "She Used to Smile Before the War": "The state robbed us of even the spaces to think about the future."

Violence became inescapable. Omar Baca writes of its maddening rhythm throughout the city, the factorylike pace that ordered urban life as he was graduating from high school and getting ready to enroll in public university in Ciudad Juárez. Initial terror gave way to hopelessness, he says, and hopelessness soon became indifference. Fabiola Román attended so many funerals she lost count of them. Bloody messages on corpses or walls alerted the population about turf struggles that spilled over entire neighborhoods. But among it all, there it was, as Miguel Salerio put it: the "punctuality of the killing." Indeed, "there was always someone killing and someone dying, always," confirms Marco Antonio López Romero, succinctly. Death as a giant clock hanging from the sky, measuring the time of the mortals.

Women faced especially strenuous circumstances. It did not take long for Marina Chávez Barrón to become aware that walking alone in Ciudad Juárez was a dangerous feat. Attending school. Going to work. Running. Visiting friends. Grocery shopping. All seemingly harmless daily activities became time bombs, massacres waiting to happen, if carried out by a woman's body. Walking as a woman implied a risk. "Fear seeps in through an invisible hole, it then shakes up all you are, and becomes you, becomes us, and then we tiptoe, evading the places you know you have to evade, averting your eyes from scenes you know you have to avert, dodging conversations you know you have to dodge, and then we embrace fear, hoping that by crying, we can console ourselves, that by taking care of each other, we can console ourselves." Fear, too, is brought to bear in Karen Cano's account in "These Daily Days," as she recalls the night her family was forced to leave her home for good. "Fear became something we experienced on a daily basis. And in my memory, the enemy was always wearing a police or army uniform." If homes became impromptu jails, the city was a mined territory on which it was better to tread carefully. Women learned this at an early age, and they knew all too well that hanging out with friends or walking by themselves, especially at night, was a matter of life or death. Poet Susana Chávez, who refused to live as a prisoner in Ciudad Juárez, was murdered in 2011, her right hand amputated. Perhaps that's the reason why Jazmín Cano chose to offer an untitled black block of ink as her testimony, quoting Mexican writer Rosa Beltrán in her epigraph: "In a country skilled in the recollection of corpses, I do [not] collect words."

I have recently gone back to Juaritos, as locals endearingly call Ciudad Juárez, on several occasions. Traces of violence still proliferate in a city trying to leave the war behind: dilapidated houses, empty lots, boarded-up buildings. Stories of youth lost to war abound among people attending readings or creative writing workshops. And yet, alongside the sorrow and the endless grieving, something akin to a sense of purpose, to a determination beyond belief, emerges on populous streets and in public gatherings. Men and women remember the lives lost and in weeping for them, in offering and welcoming condolences, they conjure their presence wherever they go. A trail of apparitions tracks their daily motions—waking up, brushing their teeth, getting dressed, taking public transportation, having lunch, looking into mirrors are all occasions for an encounter with their dead. This is how enlarging emotional communities become otherworldly and earthbound at once. They don't forget the culprits either, the state and the cartels, and a neoliberal regime that used them as cannon fodder in exchange for maximum profit. Will there ever be restitution? Will things ever change? The feminist organizations that have invited me to talk or teach in Juárez are very clear about it: things have changed only minimally, but they will take in any transformation, however miniscule. Slowly but surely, women are playing increasingly relevant roles in a city that assaulted them with particular viciousness. They are speaking up and organizing themselves against the patriarchal rule that fueled the femicide machine. They are occupying greater spaces in the cultural life of a town where male control over public readings, literary teaching posts, and publications went unchallenged. Women have become increasingly vociferous, so much so that they have often been called feminazis, a label most carry with pride (and with knowing humor). Hilda Sotelo, prominent among them, has invested countless hours in unearthing and collecting the yet unpublished poems by longtime friend Susana Chávez. Soon, or as soon as the COVID-19 pandemic allows it, *Primera tormenta* (*First Storm*) will be out by Canal Press, an independent publishing house at the University of Houston.

There is more movement in a city threatened by war in Mexico than in an average city in the United States after working hours. The use of public space is defended inch by inch, ceded only in extreme cases. Juaritos is not an anomaly: if you didn't know anything about the recent history of the city, you would have to think twice about the war that is still being waged on its streets and peripheries and homes. In recalling his years growing up in Ciudad Juárez, Omar Baca writes that "history threw at us an urgency we didn't even know how to interpret." Years later, that urgency lingers, but more men and women are ready to interpret and contest its legacy. If he were to meet Paul Nizan at one of those taco stands in downtown Juaritos, I am sure Omar would nod graciously, admitting that the French poet was right, that these were not the best years of his life. But at least they were his, I imagine him saying. The years, and the rage, and the learning.

What Countries Are These, Agripina?

VII

On *2501 Migrants* by Alejandro Santiago

1

Thousands of years ago, in what is now the Chinese city of Xi'an, an emperor, making preparations for his death and trying to extend his reign into the next life, ordered his craftsmen to reproduce a life-size statue of every soldier in his army. Using locally sourced materials and well-organized work crews, the artists not only gave each piece a unique face, thus giving them unique identities, but also placed weapons corresponding to their military rank in their hands. The realistic effect of the assembled statues was such that, years after the hated emperor Qin's death, a peasant mob attacked the terracotta soldiers, disarming and, you could say, lethally wounding many of them.

Walking among the statues that Alejandro Santiago and his team of thirty-two artisan-laborers have created in the last six years in their ranch-workshop El Zopilote, located in Santiago Suchilquitongo, a community close to the tumultuous state capital of Oaxaca, causes a similar sensation: that of finding yourself shoulder to shoulder with strangely lifelike beings that, at any moment—preferably between sips of mezcal—could begin telling you their stories about crossing the border. Simultaneously fantastic and terrifying, as fragile as the material they're made of, yet solid in the space they occupy and the air that surrounds them, Santiago's migrants cross one border above all: the thin, brittle line we often call reality.

"Sometimes I look at them from far away," says Santiago in his traveler's voice, which sounds as if it's sliding along a dirt floor, "and it seems like they're chatting." Placed around the grounds of the ranch-workshop, whether on hills or along a path, it's clear that the migrants prudently observe everything. Of human proportions and with faces that don't depict but rather evoke a reality as much internal as external, the statues aren't only a part of the landscape; they are an integral part of daily conversation. "This is a little boy about twelve years old; he's healthy, but he took a spill," Santiago half whispers while pointing gravely to one statue's broken leg. With their own stories, their own identities, these clay bodies might even evoke fear in the viewer. You could easily imagine a migration officer, years after the death of the hated emperor, holding up one of these clay migrants at gun point, a look of shock on the statue's face, tattoos of the Virgin of Guadalupe on their back, as they try to cross the border again, always again, that misunderstood mutable line both uniting and dividing the richest country in the world and its poor neighbor to the south; the nightmare and the dream; that which leaves and that which is about to leave; the here and now, and the beyond.

2

Each of Alejandro Santiago's clay migrants carries a signature. You can see it on each statue's foot. Not all of these signatures belong to Alejandro Santiago. Each signature—a curved line that extends to the ankle, a symmetrical fissure between the toes, or the faint impression of a nail—is a marker of the artist's identity: evidence that it was made by one of the thirty-two young Mixes and Mestizos who, thanks to working with Santiago, haven't had to emigrate north like so many others. Earning an average of 3,600 pesos a month—a reasonable amount in a rural region where water is scarce—the workers and even Santiago's family members are able to claim their own pieces without unnecessary fanfare or drama. To confirm the artist's identity, you simply need to examine the feet.

In his *Economic and Philosophic Manuscripts of 1844*, a young Karl Marx elaborates with characteristic passion on the labor processes created by a capitalist economy.[1] The ill-tempered young man argued that labor, by transforming the natural into the social, is the one and true source of our humanity. That is to say, in an ideal society—one in which labor and its products still belong to the worker—to work and to create would be one and the same thing, one and the same process. In such a society, a worker could pronounce, just like Santiago's sister-in-law did as she stood before a group of twelve half-completed statues: "These are mine." Her assertion's natural, unwavering tone forces us to reconsider the limits of our concept of authorship.

More than products of labor, Alejandro Santiago's 2,501 migrants *are* labor, the process in and of itself. With Zoila Santiago, the artist's wife, who organizes the administrative side of things, the artisans put as much care into constructing these clay bodies as they do tending the ranch's cows, sheep, and turkeys, which observe the finished clay statues indifferently as they flit back and forth among the fields. The artisans mix the material stored in sacks at one end of the workshop, and through trial and error—and always under Santiago's direction—choose a position that enables the clay migrants to stand on their own two feet. When a piece is ready, the artisans then place it in the kiln, where it acquires the consistency and color of a human body. The artisans also have access to the musical instruments that Santiago has collected with the hope of one day forming a norteño band.

The workshop is a cross between an agora and a small non-profit business, and its creation of clay migrants challenges—and by challenging, questions—how actual flesh-and-blood migrants are produced. If the former responds to the human needs of the region, providing the community members with a way to remain living there—in other words, to reproduce the community—the latter responds to the needs of North American capital, which creates a diaspora that, in Oaxaca and so many other states in Mexico, has left a rosary of ghost towns in its wake. It is no mere coincidence (or, in any case, it is a *co-incident* of contemporary politics) that the original context of Santiago's project is the image of an empty plaza where the specters of bodies who once lived there glide through. Perhaps much like Juan Rulfo's character Juan Preciado, who came to Comala because he had been told that his father, a man named Pedro Páramo, lived there,[2] Alejandro Santiago set about listening to the murmurs of those who had gone and vehemently wished, as we all wish for such things, for their sudden re-appearance. From the desire to see them once more, to have them close by, elbow to elbow in the daily grind, or laughing together; from the desire, too, for justice, the clay migrants were born, one by one. In number, they are twenty-five hundred: the same number of people who died trying to cross the US-Mexico border up until the year that Santiago himself crossed through the Otay Mesa Port of Entry in Baja California. Also the same number of families that, as far as Santiago remembers, lived in his hometown. *Twenty-five hundred*, the man who sits in that ghost town's empty plaza murmurs with utmost certainty, wishing. Twenty-five hundred plus one. The

next one. Twenty-five hundred plus those Alejandro Santiago
wants to sustain in Oaxaca, with life-saving job opportunities.

In the last of the three manuscripts that Marx wrote in 1844,
the philosopher argues that the "*forming* of the five senses is a
labor of the entire history of the world down to the present."[3]
Man, it was said then, learns to see, and seeing produces both
the eye and the object that the eye sees. The same happens with
smell, taste, and touch. By passing your fingertips over the clay
bodies of Santiago's migrants, you can easily feel as though the
entire history of the world up to the present is concentrated
within that touch. There lies the politics of eternity.

3

A tumultuous beauty runs through the clay migrants that
come out of El Zopilote. More than beautiful, they are overwhelming. With clasped hands and almost mystical tattoos on
their backs, the figures of men, women, and children share a
kind of original expressionism that conveys internal conflict
and strife. There is something contained in these statues that
threatens to collapse at any moment. The clay, brought directly
from Zacatecas—another region characterized by the high
number of workers that leave for the United States—can, in
effect, become mud or dust or nothing under the fierce climate
and because of the passage of time. Slashes mark the migrants'
faces and torsos, showing how the clay, which Alejandro Santiago uses as a malleable framework, opens itself up—never to
be closed again. They are flowering wounds. Identity markers.
Maps.

Far from the realist designs crafted by Emperor Qin's artisans, the faces of Santiago's migrants seem to emerge from a
private purgatory or an unborn world. Extracted, without

a doubt, from Santiago's stunning paintings, these faces are unique, but they are, at the same time, and perhaps for the same reason, unrecognizable. Those who truly wish to see them will have to get close, shut their eyes, and open them again. Those who wish to see will have to work their way into all the textured openings of the clay and occupy the face from the inside in order to see how the statue itself is seen. These faces, as the French philosopher Emmanuel Levinas said, demand. The face claims. The face, purely by existing, elicits a response: "The free movement of presence."[4] Those who wish to see will implicate themselves.

Made of coarse textures that beg to be touched, Santiago's migrants fit into a long tradition of clay sculpture in the state of Oaxaca. Among the zoomorphic figures within which chia plants grow, and the hand-sculpted women made by Teodora Blanco, the disappeared potter from Atzompa, these clay migrants are fully at home. In fact, it wouldn't be all that strange to think that the black clay sirens and the tanguyús from Tehuantepec are a part of the same tactile, delirious universe as Alejandro Santiago's 2,501 statues. There is something hallucinatory and rebellious about them; something that captures the raucousness of communal laughter, the mass retreat from the villages. Something about them calls to mind Dr. Frankenstein who, compelled by his imagination, lost his way among trembling global borders. Something of the rigid Tula Atlante transformed into a woman. Something of a mannequin that refused its commercial calling. Something, too, of a cyborg and a mutant. Something of that alien from planet Mexico that keeps ever journeying north.

As if they are defending themselves against the invisible dangers in the air, the migrants' hands are gathered close to their chests, perhaps foreshadowing the position they will assume when—standing in empty Oaxacan plazas—they find themselves finally at rest.

4

Mike Davis, the brilliant North American critic and author of the classic *City of Quartz*, once argued that the border wall is nothing more than a horrifying political spectacle.[5] Effective only in justifying the violence of border crossings and then in reinforcing the power dynamics of US imperialism, the wall hasn't been able to do what walls are supposed to do: to suspend the flow, stop the passage, contain the material. The border wall hasn't been able to prevent the incessant crossing of people required by the economy and lifestyle of the United States. This is something that Oaxacan migrants—for whom the journey north has become, over the years and generations, a way of life for entire communities—know well. I repeat: a way of life. Confronted with the risks of moving between two countries, the difficulties inherent in exile, and the rage of their exploitation, many of these migrants, as sociologist Laura Velasco Ortiz has analyzed, have created their own forms of community organization to assert their agency in the realities created by their labor.[6] While the statistical claims about Oaxacans in the United States vary (the figures in differing sources span from 30,000 to 500,000 migrants), the majority of them are concentrated in California. Introducing not only a language, or in many cases two, but also forms of sociality and protest in the fields and cities of their northern neighbor, the Oaxacan community is part of what militants as well as analysts have named the Mexicanization of the United States— that gradual but inexorable process that provokes anxiety in so many, but anticipation in so many others.

But the strength and traditions that ensured the dignified survival of the Oaxacan people during their mass migration were only possible at the expense of their intermittent or even ghostly presence in their region of origin. Their bodies are not on the streets where they were born; or only sometimes, sudden apparitions. Their hands do not hold the tools needed to work the land in order to grow corn, agave, or beans. Their eyes do not see the rusted rims of the cars that once ran. That toy. Their feet do not feel, neither out of curiosity nor devotion, the healing waters of the Hierve el Agua—two petrified waterfalls with large quantities of calcium carbonate and two small springs of carbonated water (which turns the water a greenish-blue color). Their voices. Their echoes. Alejandro Santiago's *2501 Migrants* is, essentially, a meditation on this absence. *2501 Migrants* is a project about the reach of the absent body.

Much has been said about the nostalgia of those who leave, but rarely has anyone explored, and even less frequently with clay, the melancholy of those who remain. What do witnesses to the slow process of deterioration, the gradual configuration of ruin, the always fleeting happiness of reunion, really see? How do you experience in the flesh the process through which reality empties? When you walk through the clay bodies of the 2,501 migrants, you cannot help but feel that you are surrounded by the work of a solitary yet inventive child who constructed his own playmates purely out of desire. There is something of that childlike, voracious energy in the clay bodies' design, especially in the way that sexual organs hang or open in two. A stunning dichotomy. There is something of that frenzied, impossible energy in the clay bodies that brings the migrants themselves back to us. And in order to receive and invoke them at the same time, to continue playing this extreme game called life, Alejandro Santiago places his 2,501 migrants in the northern mountains of Oaxaca, in Teococuilco de Marcos Pérez, a town that, with their presence, which is to say their total absence, will cease to be a ghost town and will become a town of pure intervention. If that isn't the power of art, what is? If this isn't a form of resistance, what is?

5

In the long study of the personal and political dynamics of human pain that make up *The Body in Pain*, Elaine Scarry analyzes with particular care how interrogation always, out of necessity, produces a confession that the person in power wants to hear—meaning that, even when the confession is true, it will, in fact, be false. An imposture responding to an imposition. An exchange that, according to various sources, not only elicits a sense of guilt but of betrayal and, even more, self-betrayal. The border agent seeks to create a unique identity through interrogation, through constant confirmation. Acknowledging the severity of the situation, it seems to function much like Scarry's interrogations, forcing the migrant to claim they are the person listed on their ID: *I am who appears there*, the migrant must claim in the presence of their identity document. *Whoever appears there is me*, they will repeat. And all of this, even if it is sometimes true, will have to be, out of necessity because that is what the person in power wants to hear, false. An imposture responding to an imposition.

Alejandro Santiago says that he has never felt more naked than when in the presence of an immigration officer. He doesn't explicitly say that interrogation is the weapon the empire uses to harm his body, but he alludes to it. What he does say is that this is one of the reasons why his 2,501 migrants are naked: all of them are permanently there, at the port of entry, projecting their voices, responding. Right now, they are all crossing. An eternal gerund. And I, who have passed over that small stretch of land so many times and who, even now, still endures that subtle confusion and horror that provokes the need to prove who I am, who among all the *Is* am I?; I stand looking at the clay bodies, and suddenly I feel like I am one of them.

And that is when you, which is another way of saying I, see us.

VIII

Nonfiction

He says he isn't a believer but that some things have happened to him recently that are making him reconsider. He says I won't even believe him. After I insist, he says he'll tell me, but that he still isn't sure. During our next ride together, he looks at me in the rearview mirror and I can see a difference in his gaze.

Beto is a taxi driver who always takes me to the airport when I'm leaving Tijuana. As long as I've known him, which has been for quite a while, he insists that one day I will end up writing one of the stories he tells me. And he tells so many! On our trips to the airport I've become familiar, through his voice, with a certain underworld of this border town that I otherwise would never have experienced. Beto also works a lot with the women in Tijuana's red-light district, and once I shared a ride with a few, because, as he explained to me, they were in a rush. An *If you don't mind*. This time is different. Instead of beginning the story by making his characteristic racket—he usually turns up the volume on the radio as he starts talking—he avoids my gaze and even rolls up the car windows. In a moment or two I will remember how, upon climbing into the car, I had admired how clean it was, how good it smelled. Its immaculateness.

He says he picked her up, like so many others, on your average street corner. He says she had long copper hair, blue eyes, and spoke with an accent from southern Mexico. He says she was a young girl, the kind who claims they're twenty when they're barely sixteen, and that's why they're so stunning. He says the girl received a call and that, with the phone still at her ear, she told him where she was headed. He says that there, in the back seat where I was sitting, she took off her sweatpants and put on a tight dress—green, quite pretty. He says her final destination was a hotel.

Beto's stories have never given me chills before. But this one, even before hearing the ending, already makes me shudder. Suddenly I want him to be quiet. Suddenly I hope that something will happen on the road or in his head that will make him stop telling me what I know he is inevitably going to tell me. Who has lived in Mexico for the last six decades and doesn't already know the ending to this story?

He says she asked for his phone number so that, once she completed her job, he could pick her up at the same place. He says between one thing and another, they broke the ice and told each other as much as they could about themselves in one ride. He tells me this while fixing me with his troubled gaze in the rearview mirror, his eyes affected by something that in the moment I could perhaps call metaphysical. He says she never called him back.

I know he hasn't yet reached the point in his story that he really wants to share because he keeps pausing for increasingly long periods of time. We discussed this once before—something about the role of silence, of empty space, in the construction of suspense. While he's quiet I watch huge billboards pass by.

He says the next morning he learned what happened while

watching television. He repeats the same words we always hear: *found dead, strangled, unidentified body*. He says he had to answer questions at the police station. And he says the same words as always: *no identity, no family, nothing at all*.

I don't know if it's at this moment or later that the nausea starts. I don't know at what moment I realize that, just a few days ago, I read similar words about a poet and translator whose murder is still unclear: his hands and feet bound, packing tape around his head, the final blow or shot. They keep getting closer, I tell myself as I instinctively move my hand from the seat where the girl changed her clothes.

He says another day, also a weekday, something similar happened to him. He says this is the part I won't believe. He says, opening his eyes wide even though they maintain a paradoxically somber look, this time when the girl got in the car she was already on the phone. He says she sighed deeply and hesitated. He says, emboldened or concerned, out of his element either way, he told her what happened to the other girl to try and convince her not to go to the hotel alone. He says he told her: That girl was just as young as you. He says right at that moment she sat there speechless, as if struck by something divine, and then she began to ask questions. He says, despondent yet not shedding a single tear, that she told him the girl was her sister. He says she then dialed a number and in a quiet voice, quiet as a mouse, she told her mother the news. He says she said: Now I know where my sister is.

What are the chances? he asks me, as if I know. Can I not clearly see the intervention of something beyond human understanding? he insists. I don't know what to think about his religious conversion or of the gray landscape that unfolds into dust and noise on the other side of the window. Social sadness is so intimate sometimes. And intimacy can be so sad.

Carlos Beristáin, sociologist, doctor, and specialist for the Inter-American Court of Human Rights, says that violence in Mexico has reached a catastrophic level. He also says that the legacy of this violence will impact, at the very least, entire generations. The pain. The rage. The impotence.

IX

Elvira Arellano and That Which Blood, Tradition, and Community Unite

The deportation order that Elvira Arellano received on August 15, 2006, could have led to yet another of the many incidents that make up the bloody history of Mexican migration in the United States. Like so many others, Elvira entered the United States without the required documents, something that did not stop her from finding work in Oregon, where she first settled, and later in Chicago, where she moved years later, then with a son. An immigration raid at the airport where she was employed launched her journey to become one of the most important working-class leaders within the Latinx community. Unlike many others in her situation, Elvira Arellano refused to return to Mexico upon receiving a deportation order. Instead, she sought refuge in the Adalberto Memorial United Methodist Church in Chicago, where she lived for almost a year. Her actions catapulted the New Sanctuary movement, popularized in Illinois by the Methodist pastor José S. Landaverde, to new heights. From within these religious institutions, and later from the streets of the United States and Tijuana, Elvira Arellano has repeatedly asserted her message: it is necessary to establish immigration reform that respects the unity of

Mexican families that settle, or that form once they are settled, in the United States.

With precise words, often emphasizing the pronoun *we* and the word *dignity* in her speeches, Elvira Arellano did not rely on sentimentalism to express the series of events that led her from working as a manual laborer for various North American companies to becoming a social activist who addresses the Latinx community as well as members of the governments in both countries involved. Poised, drawing on her profound faith and tireless fighting spirit, Elvira made the complex realities of immigrant families evident in her speeches, especially the frequent and forced separation of parents and children, as well as the church's active role in starting a movement to offer asylum to migrants threatened with deportation.

Like the Madres de Plaza de Mayo in Argentina, Elvira Arellano has successfully utilized the concept of maternity to call on citizens as well as their representatives in Congress to approve an immigration reform capable of safeguarding the rights of workers and their families. Without opposing the state, yet compelling it to fulfill its function as protector of the well-being and rights of its constituents, Elvira appealed to her role as mother and family member to legitimize her argument. Indeed, photographs of Elvira typically include her little Saúl, who accompanied her in intimate family scenes as well as at public marches and churches. Validating herself through traditional gender roles, Elvira Arellano has shed light on an often unacknowledged yet deeply obvious truth: immigration today is not only made up of men who leave their families behind in search of work. To reflect the complexity of immigration today, we must add to this stereotype the faces of the many working-class women who cross the border to reconfigure their own family units or even to start their own families, as well as out of economic or political necessity. That was the case, in fact, for Elvira, who conceived and gave birth to Saúl, her only son, in the United States. The possibility of being separated from Saúl, something that Elvira continues to describe as unjust and, moreover, unnatural, has constituted the basis of her rejection to deportation.

Like the first uprisings that set the Mexican Revolution in motion in 1910, Elvira Arellano has also declared she would heed the laws of God, not those of men and their governments, in her search for just and dignified treatment of migrant families. She abides by a higher law—she has confirmed this several times. Following Saint Teresa of Cabora and others who embraced faith and, based on that faith, did not recognize governmental authority, Elvira Arellano demanded that "what God has united, let man not separate." Elvira thus has established herself within a long tradition of struggle legitimized through the popular appropriation of religious discourse. It is fitting, then, that she chose the sacred grounds of the church to make her social plea.

But when Elvira left the grounds of her Methodist church in Chicago to participate in various marches throughout California, neither the social importance of motherhood nor popular religion were enough to stop the immigration officers from arresting her on August 19, 2007, in Los Angeles, just outside the church on Olvera Street. It was dark when Elvira arrived in Tijuana, and there, steps away from the turnstiles that would lead this woman, born in 1975, back to her country of origin, she repeated her urgent message: she would not rest until she achieved immigration reform guaranteeing the unity of migrant families.

And rest Elvira Arellano has not. In Tijuana, she founded the Elvira Arellano Refuge House—an organization that takes in women deported from the United States while they contact their communities or seek assistance to rebuild their lives. Operating in downtown Tijuana since December 16, 2007, the Refuge House provides secular sanctuary for women who are at greater risk due to being deported at night. Aside from meeting with presidents and leading massive protests, Elvira Arellano has also run for office in Mexican elections. While in Ciudad Juárez, miles east along that same border, women are murdered and silenced, Elvira uses her voice to demand that the state can't pull apart that which blood, tradition, and community unite.

X

What Country Is This, Agripina?

The title of this essay comes from a question in "Luvina," a marvelous short story by Juan Rulfo. In the story, Agripina is the wife of an ex–rural teacher who, drinking beer after beer, narrates to another man, possibly another visitor to Luvina, how he lost his life and his dreams when he moved there, to that sad, rocky town located on the Crude Stone Hill, where relentless gusts of black wind don't even allow bittersweet grow.

According to the man who tells the story of his time in Luvina, and for whom telling it is a sort of camphor rinse for his head, one fine day he found himself there along with his family. Then, clearly overwhelmed by the town's strangeness, perhaps foreshadowing both his future and our own, the man asks his wife:

"What country are we in, Agripina?"[1]

And it's there, in the town plaza—a word that comes from the Latin *plattea* and that indeed once meant, according to the *Real Academia Española* dictionary, "wide and spacious place within a town, toward which various streets tend to flow," but now we know well that it is the turf of a drug cartel—that Agripina gives her succinct, mute, monumental response:

"And she shrugged her shoulders."[2]

I am part of a generation that was born just after the so-called Mexican miracle, growing up—this was, in fact, the miracle—over the following decades: years of crisis and insolence, rampant corruption and economic decline. I even lived through, for example, the devaluation that doubled the peso from 12.50 to one American dollar to 25. Not to mention all the other devaluations, witnessing how exchange rates and prices reached laughable sums that included more zeros than you could count. Purely by chance, I attended a free concert that Rockdrigo, not yet the brilliant, gritty rock singer of our generation, gave on my college campus for a small group of students to whom he made all the sense in the world. I was there, in every meaning of the word, when the 1985 earthquake ravaged Mexico City hours later. I learned, with rage and frustration, about the selective repressions mandated under the Salinas administration, and I continue to follow the deaths of journalists and social activists today. Like many in the mideighties, I emigrated north because, for a graduate of the Universidad Nacional Autónoma de México with a degree in sociology, the prospects for a life in a country clearly turning toward neoliberalism were few. To put it mildly, the violence of our contemporary history has never been foreign to me. Nevertheless, during all those years, it rarely occurred to me to ask the question that the narrator poses to Agripina, his wife, barely a moment after arriving in Luvina.

But years pass (as narrators tend to observe), and reality

(voracious and unjust, as it has always been) has become increasingly strange for me. In light of the students murdered with impunity in Ciudad Juárez, and more recently in Monterrey, the same question: What country are we in, Agripina? In light of an illegitimate war organized by a president who values his political legitimization more than the well-being and safety of the civil population, the same question: What country are we in, Agripina?

In Juan Rulfo's story, Agripina shrugs her shoulders once more after leaving a church that she entered simply to pray. Then, slowly, between swallows of beer, the ex–rural teacher starts to describe Luvina: it is a sad place, that we already know, where only "old people . . . and those who aren't yet born"[3] live—and the dead, of course, our dead. Later, about to start in on some mezcal, the man recalls the only time he saw the people of Luvina smile. It was when he suggested they look for a better place to live and he told them that the government would even help them do so. Far from shrugging their shoulders, they let out a chilling laugh and answered:

> "We know it [the government], too. It so happens that we do. What we know nothing about is the government's mother."[4]

This phrase speaks volumes. But here I am, in the middle of another plaza where everything swirls around me and exposes the open. There is the open. Here it is. I do not write as a political analyst, because I am not one. I write from further within. I write as what I manage to sometimes be: a writer. What country is this, Agripina? you ask me from so far away. It is the country we became, Juan. Perhaps by staying silent. Perhaps by not listening to the voices of the dead. Perhaps by looking away. Perhaps our name is Indolence.

XI

Cacaluta

We tread on dry leaves. We walk over yellow and green and brown leaves. We turn away from the sidewalk. Turn away from the sound. The human settlements. Now we walk over the leaves of the low forest. The deciduous forest. Our feet make noise against the leaves. Against the fallen branches, our feet prompt the sound of something breaking. Something that snaps. We go down the trail. We slowly amble along the trail that's called Sicarú in Zapotec, that means *hermosa* in Spanish, *beautiful* in English. This is a place where trees are revered. Here the land slopes up, leading to a tree. Huatulco, that's the place you mean.

Now we walk over the wet leaves that cover Sicarú. Step by step, we amble along. Toward the lagoon, we amble along. With measured breath, we amble along. Toward the smell of earth mixed with centuries-old water. That mud. That clay. Toward the shore, so smooth. The beating of a heron's wings breaks the calm in two. Then an egret's. The stilts with their long red feet wade through the water and the brown-feathered boobies swoop over it, feeding. From afar, a vermilion flycatcher looks like a flower or a flame. Red against dark green. Red against emerald green. This is the grackle's lagoon. This is a wetland.

A pink-colored spoonbill alights on the water. Another egret. A magpie. A stork. The delicate and curved bills of the avocets hunt for invertebrates.

The sound of our footsteps on leaves. The sound of branches snapping. The beating of an oriole's wings. A yellow wing flaps within the foliage of the mangroves. Another magpie. A cacique. Birdsong, their cries. The way in which they call to one another. We are in front of the pochote, the tree. The deer feed from its trunk, beaded with small droplets of water. From its fruit, so sweet. Using its seeds, which fall like leaves over Sicarú, you can make a pillow—rest your ear on them and dream about the tropical forest. About the trail. We amble along under the termite nests. Under the vines. Under the branches that, seen from below, transfigure the map of the heavens. A falcon. A vulture. The squawks of the chachalacas.

We are in front of the huanacaxtle. In front of its immense trunk. In front of its roots that come out of the earth and bury themselves again in search of water from the lagoon. We are underneath its foliage. And we touch its skin. From this bark, crushed, soap is made to wash clothes or tan leather. From among its leaves, which stay glued to the branch for eight months, will spring brown, ear-shaped pods. The tree that listens: the huanacaxtle. The ancestral tree. Here, below, among the undergrowth along the trail, are holes dug by skunks. Here, in another season, reptiles lay their eggs. This is the cuachalalate, the tree whose bark, when made into a tea, can cure gastritis. We stop. The sounds of our steps over the leaves stop.

The birds of prey will arrive soon, in November. The migration will begin. The ospreys. The hawks. Their wings extended against the sky. Their shadows against the wild agave. Against the Siracú trail. Then come the other birds. Thousands of other birds. The ducks. The wings. The feathers. Their feet in the shallow lagoon. Their songs among the ficus amazquite and the ficus insipida. Their shadows against the huayacán, a tree that is more a bush when it's near the coast. And it crawls there, on the coast, its branches on the sand. Its two-hundred-year-old branches on the sand. We amble along, now over the sand. One step and then another, sinking into the sand. The rosadía has thorns on its leaves. The copal tree has a yellow-colored lichen that stains its trunk, its giant thorns. These are the parts of a cactus that are no longer green but red, that flower. Yellow and round and delicate, the nopal flower in the sand. Like our steps, on the sand. In the sand. Sinking.

We are on the sand. Before the emerald-green and bottle-green and seafoam-green water, pacific-green water. Before the navy-blue and royal-blue and bluest-blue water. Other blues with no name. We are under the celestial vault. There go the breakers over the schools of skipjacks and tuna and sardines. There goes the flight of the vulture. That, moving swiftly, is an osprey. Someone will surely catch a flying fish or a marlin this year. Someone will cast a hook like the others, like so many, but instead of catching a common fish, an enormous, iridescent fish will come out of the Pacific waters. We see all of this. We can see and walk among it all. We breathe. We give thanks.

Huatulco means "the place where you pay tribute to the trees."

All of it, the deciduous low forest that surrounds the Bay of Cacaluta, right where fresh water from the heart of the forest spills, is threatened by the Federal Electricity Commission, who are constructing a power plant. All those birds, all those leaves, all those tree trunks, all those years turned into energy and chlorophyll and air, all those migrations, all those footsteps on leaves; all drowned out by the noise of the machines that chop down trees and split the earth in two, into pieces.

XII

Desiccated Mermaids

Bernardino de Sahagún, the Franciscan friar who arrived in New Spain in 1529, was prone to climb mountains and dive into lakes and rivers. Little in his official portrait as an amateur ethnologist and dedicated scholar—the author of the monumental *General History of the Things of New Spain* (also known as the *Florentine Codex*)—betrays such penchant for strenuous physical activity and the outdoors. But he did famously hike up Popocatépetl and Iztaccíhuatl, the snow-capped volcanoes that can easily be seen from Mexico City on a clear day. Once, he hurled himself into Xochimilco in an attempt to retrieve an idol from under the water and replace it with a Catholic stone cross. In book 11 he describes the volcano Xinantecatl, the pre-Hispanic Nahuatl toponym for the Nevado de Toluca, specifically the two lakes that ripple in its elliptical crater some 13,800 feet above sea level, naming the highlands, plains, and slopes; the diversity of waters and the quality and dispositions of the earth; the forests and gardens of his lifelong work:

> There is another body of water, where they were also accustomed to sacrifice, which is in the province of Toluca near

the village of Calimanyan. It is a high mountain which has two springs on top which flow nowhere. The water is very clear and nothing lives in it because it is very cold. One of these springs is very deep. A great number of offerings appear therein. . . . This was in the year 1570, or near then.[1]

Some five hundred years later, the water at this altitude is still very cold and the Sun and Moon Lakes, those mile-wide springs nestled in the crater of the volcano, still attract pilgrims and believers who, due to the low amount of oxygen in the atmosphere, arrive at their shores literally out of breath, altitude sickness piercing their heads. Sheltered by the volcano's peak and exhausted by their effort, the pilgrims pause. An arid blue sky just barely separates them from outer space. The waters, still clear all these years later, call to them. Something is moving down there, below the otherwise calm surface. Something threatens to jump into their laps.

The presence of mermaids in the traditional iconography and in the many legends that surround the highlands of central Mexico is surprising, if not completely shocking. It's not natural or logical, after all, to picture these extraordinary beings so far from the sea, especially in a landscape dominated by mountains and forests, plows and furrows. But despite this, you hear of mermaids and mermen everywhere, living happily in the icy waters of the Sun and Moon Lakes, for example, both located in the crater of a volcano.

The age-old way of life in this lacustrine region has been lost forever. But the Nevado de Toluca remains a sacred territory since at least the fifteenth and sixteenth centuries. Priests, visionaries, pilgrims, and believers would all travel to the two lakes situated at the mountain's peak, which the locals call the "two eyes of the sea." Each group of visitors would leave their mark: meaningful offerings of copal or agave leaves, which have been slowly unearthed and investigated by teams of underwater archeologists from the Universidad Nacional Autónoma de México. Scepters, many shaped like lightning bolts, also abound in this place. For both the ancient and current inhabitants of the Toluca Valley, the mountain acts like a large "glass of water" that, thanks to lightning and sometimes aided by graniceros, or hail healers, pour their precious waters into the surrounding regions. In rural societies, whose physical and spiritual survival depend primarily on growing corn, this has been a matter of the upmost importance.

For those who live in this area of Mexico, it is easy to believe in the existence of a network of streams and underground rivers that start at the volcano's peak and eventually connect with distant seas and oceans. In fact, throughout the twentieth century up until the fateful day of June 23, 1950, all aspects of daily life in the valley were influenced by three great lakes: Chignahuapan, Chimaliapan, and Chiconahuapan. The riverside villagers in the municipalities of Ocoyoacac and Tultepec to Almoloya, Atizapán, and Texcalyacac were mostly fishermen or tuleros who lived off trout, frogs, and crayfish, and depended on the lakes for their very survival. But all of that disappeared, all at once, on that fateful day when the waters of the Lerma River were diverted to meet the needs of Mexico City. One stormy night, a group of engineers destroyed the springs in the region, cutting off the water supply to the river. The people remember. When the lakes dried up, when the marshes were turned into a reservoir, the legends of vengeful, threatening mermaids took on greater strength in the region.

At the beginning of the twenty-first century, the researchers José Antonio Trejo Sánchez and Emilio Gerardo Arriaga conducted a series of interviews with the inhabitants of the Toluca Valley. In the words of one villager, Atanasio Serrano:

> In the year 1950, in the month of June, on the Feast of Corpus Christi, the river was lost forever. The people living along the shore said that one night after a downpour with a lot of lightning they heard a sound, as if the land were sucking something up, and they realized that at that moment the engineers were testing the pumps installed in El Cero. The next day the lake turned to mud; the water lilies and tules faded away, and thousands of aquatic species were buried in sludge. The waters that gave life to the famous Lerma River were no more.[2]

Among all the interviews conducted, one about the Atlanchane or "lake mermaid" stands out. A villager, Cerón Hernández, recounts a conversation he had:

> It was an elderly man, some eighty years old, who told me everything.
>
> "Excuse me, is that someone crying in Agua Blanca?" I asked him.
>
> "Yes, son, yes, she is crying. Do you know why? Because they killed the merman, the mermaid's husband."
>
> "How did they kill him?"
>
> "Yes, look, there was a lot of blood, like a two-meter radius in the water."
>
> "Oh really?"
>
> "And we did not find him."
>
> "Well then, what happened to him?"
>
> "Well, that señorita pulled him under the surface, because there was a really deep spring over there, I believe as deep as from this corner to San Sebastián; *that* deep. Well, overnight all the fish just disappeared, señor. There were some left, but very few—and no more mermaids or anything. It was over. What happened to them? God only knows."
>
> Then came the construction . . .[3]

Every time someone in Mexico City turns on their kitchen or bathroom sink, the water levels drop a little more. But perhaps the voices—and warnings—of the mermaids travel in that same torrent of water, telling all those city dwellers that, although desiccated, although apparently gone, they refuse to leave what is left of the lakes.

XIII

The Morning After

It's a gray morning in the Second Ward, the historically Mexican neighborhood in Houston, Texas. It's also a crushingly silent morning. The neighbor across the street, the one who regularly comes outside shirtless to hang clothes on the laundry line, has broken his routine—he does not come outside this morning. The sounds of motors, or of footsteps outside, cannot be heard either. Car radios, which frequently invade the neighborhood with songs or interviews, have fallen silent. The empty streets, lined with tall, immobile walnut trees, let the cold wind that announces the still-subtle impending presence of winter blow through as it pleases. It's a war zone. Like an area ravaged by war, where everything has been lost. It is the morning of November 9, 2016, and Donald Trump has won, against almost all expectations, the presidency of the United States.

What does it feel like? Fucked up—that's how it feels.

There are other questions that arise, still silent, when faces eventually begin to appear on sidewalks, at bus stops, in classrooms and offices. That hidden vulnerability of those who know they have been exposed. The look of someone who still doesn't fully understand. My colleagues, my fellow professors, my neighbors, the people I encounter every morning or every evening: Did they vote against me? The question could be innocent if it weren't so terrifying. The middle- and upper-middle-class white vote—by white men and women with and without education, open to anything that will preserve their privilege—responds that yes, indeed, they voted against you. The vote of the white working class, too, who saw their jobs in heavy industry disappear as NAFTA was established, and with it, the fierce sequel to neoliberalism, answers: Yes, I voted against you. What are we going to do when we run into each other at grocery stores and banks, at parent meetings, outside of schools, at the gym? How are we going to be able to look each other in the eye knowing what we know now, what has become chillingly clear to both of us?

Because one thing is obvious: the ethnic and racial diversity of the United States is irreversible. We are going to continue to see ourselves and find ourselves in the same places where, until today, a sociality has been performed that, like any community, is sometimes messy, sometimes tentative, frequently inharmonious, but always dynamic. The almost fifteen million Latinxs that, according to census data, live in California have been a demographic majority since July 1, 2015, and they are not going to cease to exist. And would it be better for us to leave? asks my son who, yesterday, with all his friends, went out to vote to support, among other things, the legalization of recreational marijuana. And I don't hesitate to tell him no. To tell him we are staying. To tell him this has been our country for at least three generations. To tell him we have the right to have as happy and full a life as anyone else. To tell him that, instead of thinking about fleeing, let's think about building. To tell him we have to protect our strengths and get in touch with our people to continue forming lively, persistent communities.

And this is what we do at the office where, on that morning, we all arrive with our eyes still brimming with fear, reflecting both the nightmare and the reality. We convene an emergency meeting to plan the strategies we will have to implement if we want our projects and programs to continue to receive the resources we have won thanks to the battles of entire generations of Mexicans, Mexican Americans, Latinxs, and Chicanxs who made our university a Hispanic-serving institution. The terror is stifling, but we find encouragement in the speed with which ideas arise and the urgency with which everyone fulfills their tasks, as if time were running out and our lives were on the line.

Time is running out and our lives are on the line.

Or perhaps it is the other way around: perhaps time is just beginning and our lives have just begun. I've never had much confidence in a democracy of the powerful for the powerful. And I am convinced that the neoliberal devotion to profit is shared with greater or lesser cynicism by both parties in contention. What we lose in this moment of unmasking is not democracy or equality but the false notion that the best part of a bad deal is still worth your while. When the enemy's face is revealed in such an obvious way, when things are named without any tact and without the veil of good manners, it is the moment to show our true face as well. It's called living in resistance. It's called searching among the desolation of the morning after, turning to others to imagine the unimaginable: the world we want to live in.

Hard times are coming for us, indeed. But also for them.

XIV

On Our Toes: Women against the
Mexican Femicide Machine

Young Mexican women are enraged. And rightfully so. According to official SESNSP statistics from 2019, ten women are killed and 4,320 are raped in Mexico on a daily basis. They disappear on dusty roads in the hinterland. They text desperate cries for help after being abducted in taxi cabs. They post warnings about their executioners on Facebook. They stand in long lines to file legal charges against their abusers, to no avail. They go missing in crowded neighborhoods or faraway towns. They are there and suddenly they aren't. A murderous flickering. Their body parts painstakingly described on the news: *a severed head, two legs, a hand.* Meanwhile, they are sorely missed in offices and classrooms, at parties and family reunions. Their absence constitutes the black hole of a nation gone awry.

The war on women first appeared in newspaper headlines in the late twentieth century, when tales of Ciudad Juárez, that notorious border town, familiarized us with the term *femicide.* Unsuspecting audiences thus learned that dark-skinned and long-haired women working at assembly plants were bodies at great risk. From that point on, concomitant to the terror, human rights organizations emerged to demand justice: Norma Andrade and Marisela Ortiz Rivera consolidated their efforts, forming Nuestras Hijas de Regreso a Casa A.C., a civil organization that searches for missing women when authorities desist or fail to do so. Justicia para Nuestras Hijas was the grassroots group that worked closely with Marisela Escobedo Ortiz to demand justice for her daughter's femicide in 2008. Marisela was later killed on the streets of Chihuahua in 2010. The mothers of Ciudad Juárez, much like their predecessors during the military dictatorships in Argentina or Chile, joined forces to urge the state to fulfill its duty: to protect and preserve the safety of its citizens. Rampant impunity, corruption at all levels of government, and a strongly held patriarchal ideology, however, has fueled the ceaseless killing of women from all walks of life.

Despite increasing violence, *feminism* has remained an f-word in Mexican vocabularies. Well into the twenty-first century, many intellectuals—both men and women—have generally despised or unabashedly rejected feminist ideas, arguing that they were either unnecessary for a world that had achieved acceptable levels of equality or were too extreme—a matter better left to crazy women in need of discipline. Having grown up fearing for their lives, young women from Mexico think otherwise. And they have acted accordingly. In early August 2019, as authorities failed to apprehend four police officers accused of raping a seventeen-year-old girl, contingents of outraged women who proudly identified themselves as feminists descended on the prosecutor's office, clamoring for a meeting with the city's district attorney. Banners with phrases like "They don't protect me, they rape me" and "If you violate women, we will violate your laws" abounded on-site. Then, as a security officer attempted to assure women the case would be properly investigated, he was glitter bombed. Images of the officer's head, doused in pink glitter, captured national and international attention. A new phase of women's mobilization against gender violence in Mexico had begun, but the revolution had been unleashed years earlier.

In July 2015 Mexican feminist poets Maricela Guerrero, Paula Abramo, and Xitlálitl Rodríguez Mendoza launched the hashtag #RopaSucia (#DirtyLaundry) to showcase incidences of misogyny in academic institutions and cultural circles. "Do you remember a misogynous comment from an artist, an editor, a writer, a cultural bureaucrat? Send them to us. Let's start dancing," Guerrero tweeted on July 13, 2015. And dance they did. Rebelling against the well-known Mexican saying "La ropa sucia se lava en casa"—which demands decorum from women, metaphorically asking them to do their laundry within the privacy of their home—Guerrero and a surprising number of women opted for airing their dirty secrets in public instead. "Poetry written by women is not as good as poetry written by men in the Spanish-speaking world" was perhaps the most retweeted of responses, along with: "Your writing is so good it almost looks like a man's writing" and "You might not be a good fit for this grant because you're pregnant." Something happens when open secrets—ones we all know about and discreetly share—are enunciated in public. They lose their spell, their capacity for stupor or paralysis. Supporters of #RopaSucia not only unveiled the complicity of perpetrators, but in showing how gender discrimination can be cloaked within concrete words and human stories, they forced others to acknowledge its very existence. Gender violence could no longer be the elephant in the room.

A year later, under the hashtag #MiPrimerAcoso (#MyFirst-Assault), women of all ages continued airing the deepest secrets of patriarchy. Memories of sexual harassment painfully uncovered the makings of a machista system that terrorizes girls early in life, forcing them into silence and submission thereafter. From harassment to rape, women's stories depicted families in turmoil, workspaces riddled with violence, and public spaces where women are more often than not merely prey. Candid and sordid, these 140-character stories hit a nerve. As with #RopaSucia, the sheer number of participants in #MiPrimerAcoso made clear that many skeletons were in the closet, ready to burst out. The unsettling truth that emerged from these accounts was that the violence that gave way to femicides was not an exception but the rule in many of these women's lives. The child molester, the abusive husband, the vicious boss, the rapist, and the murderer are not monsters lurking in the outskirts of cities and villages but "normal" men allowed to threaten and kill women simply because they can. Impunity cements the deadly contract that keeps women in their place—the kitchen or the coffin. Silence seals the patriarchal pact that keeps men on top.

Once again, in March 2019, Mexican feminist writers and artists joined forces to break the silence surrounding sexual abuse and gender discrimination in workplaces and literary circles. Embracing the methods of #MeToo movements around the world and skillfully using social media, middle-class women of younger generations not only painted frightful scenarios where women were humiliated and torn apart on a regular basis but for the first time they were willing to name names. On Twitter. And the debate around gender inequality and the femicide machine took on an unexpectedly vociferous and increasingly divisive turn from there. As feminist organizers called for and disseminated accusations shared anonymously—although, as they explained later, generated in communities of trust—readers, both men and women, reacted with mounting unease and, eventually, wrath.

Most people who acknowledge violence against women have generally accepted that rapists and killers are deranged men from the working classes or unhinged men from organized-crime ranks, but the names that the Mexican #MeToo movement aired in public belonged to well-known figures from prominent backgrounds or well-educated men— authors, publishers, curators—the public was not used to fearing. The enemy, it turned out, was at home. A crude argument about the pertinence, and even the legality, of these accusations ensued, with men and even some women threatening to file charges against #MeToo organizers. Meanwhile, young women from all over Mexico sent out stories too painful to bear, overwhelming organizers and taking over the movement.

Revolutions are not orderly affairs, and this was no exception. No one raised her hand to be allowed to speak. Hastily planned assemblies emerged in Mexico City and elsewhere, where women under duress continued with the outpouring of their life stories, providing a language that triggered empathy, bewilderment, identification, and in some cases, animosity. As women read other women's stories, they saw themselves in situations they had been unable to name. "So it was rape after all," some of them tweeted, both baffled and liberated by words the patriarchy would rather have hushed: Molestation. Catcalling. Assault. Discrimination. Harassment. Domestic violence. Abuse—physical and financial. Rape. Murder. If what we knew about gender violence had previously been a portolano—a medieval map only outlining the coasts—each story told by these women was now presenting the dreadful details of the inland. The map filled in from these broken silences configured a veritable heart of darkness, and it was not a flattering sight. Some men apologized, making acts of public contrition, including the promise to seek professional help. Others didn't even acknowledge the accusations against them. Some were fired from their jobs. Some threatened revenge. But in April 2019, the suicide of famous Mexican singer Armando Vega Gil, accused of child molestation, brought the movement to an abrupt halt.

Vega Gil's suicide letter encapsulated the turmoil many men in Mexico were experiencing. On one hand, Vega Gil—who first became a star as a member of the rebellious and peripatetic rock band Botellita de Jerez—expressed his desperate conviction that the anonymous accusation was going to ruin a career that, in recent years, had included writing children's books. On the other, he condemned violence against women, wholeheartedly supporting women's rights. While the conservative reaction speedily blamed feminists for the suicide, prompting women to keep their mouths shut, members of Vega Gil's band were swift in their support for the movement, issuing a joint condemnation against gender violence. April became the cruelest of months. The movement looked inward, in a feverish soul-searching that involved the self-care and safety of its members as well as discussion around the steps that awaited the movement's future. Feminist collectives materialized across the country, creating discussion cells on issues ranging from public policy to self-defense. As their exchanges remained concealed from public view, it all seemed quiet on the surface. Beneath it all, boiling with fury and tenacity, women were more determined than ever to achieve justice.

Meanwhile, the war on women persisted. Newspapers featured the usual somber news with characteristic ease, and gruesome murders alerted the population to the unquestionable reach of machismo and impunity. So when the authorities of Mexico City failed to even address rape accusations against police officials, women armed with telling banners and pink glitter returned to the streets on August 12, and then again four days later. And they were taking no prisoners. Perhaps more commonly associated with arts-and-crafts assignments, elementary school projects, or outrageous partying, pink glitter took on a new political dimension alongside the radical wing of the LGBTQ movement in the early twenty-first-century United States. Glitter bombing is not only visually striking as it identifies and publicly shames the enemy; it's also force free. In the hands of feminist protesters, pink glitter became a vivid reminder that women's patience had been tested to the limits and that direct action was the next step in a mounting struggle that would define the heart of the nation.

As with Argentine activists associated with the #MareaVerde (#GreenTide) movement to defend abortion rights, it is clear that young Mexican women are no longer shy about defining themselves as feminists. And as with younger activists around the world, Mexican women are not afraid to leave their marks on walls and monuments. The Ángel de la Independencia, a phallic statue crowned with a golden angel that celebrates Mexican independence on Reforma Avenue, now bears the traces of women's fury. From "We will cut off your penises" to "While you complain about the graffiti: ten women are killed and 4,320 are raped each day, which side are you on?" feminist activists are posing questions the country cannot ignore. The government of Andrés Manuel López Obrador, who was elected by a landslide in 2018, has sent mixed signals so far. In an attempt to curb corruption, he has defunded women's shelters as well as nurseries and day-care centers, supporting women's and families' direct access to state resources instead. Claudia Sheinbaum, the mayor of Mexico City, described the

August mobilizations as mere "provocations" that her government was not going to acquiesce to, gaining immediate widespread disapproval. And members of López Obrador's cabinet have been particularly insensitive around gender issues, often portraying conventional women as role models for newer generations. But the glitter revolution is here to stay.

Today's feminism is no longer solely comprised of white intellectuals of the urban classes. Two years ago, Zapatista women successfully organized a massive feminist meeting in the Chiapas highlands, launching a national conversation about gender and Indigenous rights. Indigenous activists and scholars such as Yásnaya Elena Aguilar and Gladys Tzul Tzul have worked relentlessly in desedimenting the racial layers of gender oppression. Furious and levelheaded, able to forge dialogues with and within Indigenous and working-class communities, these twenty-first-century feminists are intersectional, equally interested in issues of class and racial discrimination as well as in a radical critique of the ravages of late neoliberalism. They know that our common enemy stems from the enclaves of extractive capitalism, patriarchy, and racism. If silence is a formidable adversary, feminists of all persuasions have been able to unearth and share a language able to name violence and voice hope, forming emotional communities that often transcend national boundaries.

Let us not forget that women in Mexico did not gain the right to vote until 1953, and that femicide as such was included in the penal code only in the summer of 2012. And while there is no turning back, it is also true that every inch of the terrain is still in dispute. As powerful as the femicide machine has proven to be, recent victories—such as the decriminalization of abortion in the state of Oaxaca, a clear win for the Mexican #MareaVerde—are a telling sign that the times may indeed be changing. But simultaneously, legislation passed in the northern state of Nuevo León may prevent the LGBTQ community's ability to secure medical care. Now more than ever, it is urgent to remain on our toes.

Under the Narco Sky

XV

Horrorism

Cf. Medea and Medusa, the gesture of the victim. The shards.

I never want to read these words again: *My son died in my arms.*

"My son died in my arms," Cinthia Salazar Castillo proclaimed.

I never want to read these words again: *The bullet was meant for me but killed my son.*

"The bullet was meant for me but killed my son," she repeated.

I never want to read these words again: *They were soldiers, all in uniforms.*

"They were soldiers, all in uniforms," the family's mother reported.

And the resurrection?

"They were minutes filled with terror, fear, courage,"
she repeated over and over.
"They were minutes filled with terror, fear, courage,"
she repeated over and over.
"They were minutes filled with terror, fear, courage,"
she repeated over and over.
"They were minutes filled with terror, fear, courage,"
she repeated over and over.

The result: Two dead boys. High-caliber firearms. Easter
Sunday.

The word: *shard*. The words.

They began to shoot and shoot and shoot.

While the violence invades and acquires unprecedented
forms, contemporary language has difficulty giving it
plausible names: Martín and Bryan Almanza; Nuevo
Laredo–Reynosa–Matamoros.

An ontology of vulnerability: that which exposes us to the
dependency of the other; for their care as much as their
outrage.

Someone bleeds out on the mountain. Someone breathes,
terrified. Someone is afraid.

The word: *shard*. The words.

They began to shoot and shoot and shoot.

I never want to read these words again: *They began to shoot and shoot and shoot.* I never want to read the word *unarmed.*

"I told the one who was pointing his gun at me to kill me, that two of my five children were already dead," the mother recalls.

I never want to read these words again: *They kept launching grenades at us.*

"They kept launching grenades at us," she says.

The mother's face, chest, and arms still bear traces of the shards.

The word *unarmed.* The gesture of the victim.

A vigil is held for two white coffins containing the remains of Bryan and Martín in the modest home at 1135 Calle Esfinge in the crowded community of Los Colorines.

An ontology of vulnerability, the human condition that exposes us to the dependency of the other; for their care as much as their outrage.

XVI

The War We Lost

Whenever I'm in Tijuana, I eat at a taco truck called El Chapo—their tacos de cazón a la plancha are the best in town. Military checkpoints are a common sight in this cantankerous city, where I spend two weeks every month. Often, I am forced to the side of the road by convoys driven by men in military gear. Their AK-47s pointing outward. Their faces covered by black masks. We have grown accustomed to the piercing sound of police sirens as they hurry through streets and back alleys, chasing pickups with tinted windows. When the sirens die down, a rare occurrence, the sound of the ocean—crashing waves, distant caws of seagulls, wind currents—reminds us that Tijuana is a city by the sea. Some of my family members report even more alarming news from the other corner of the country in Tamaulipas: curfews, recess cancelations, empty restaurants, roads on which no one dares travel. All this, since always. An *always* defined, clearly, as the past six years. A little more. A little less.

We have shared the same sky for a long time now. We know about them and they know about us. As time passes, there are fewer of us. Permeability has its price. But this week, it's been more in my face than ever: on the covers of magazines, in comments sections of online newspaper articles, on my computer screen. Here they are. This is their territory. The narco. The boss's boss. The plaza, their turf. I feel them, like I rarely have before, so very close by. It could be an ekphrastic effect, given that the narco's appearances already went from indifference to hope and then fear, but the number of deaths is too real. Women, students, and now children. In *Horrorism: Naming Contemporary Violence*, Adriana Cavarero questions the glamour and mythification that typically surround the actions of the warrior.[1] Horror is too real, too messy. Very much in our faces. As insidious as grime under our fingernails. There is no stoicism to it. No glory. This is not an epic narrative. Sharing her position (few things are more tedious than the mind of a serial killer, if you ask me), I cannot help but call attention to the massive media presence of the narco. I recall the message inscribed on my rearview mirror: *Objects in mirror are closer than they appear.*

I've always been reluctant to believe in heroes, especially men flashing a virility many should instantly dismiss as machismo. (I suppose this is also why I never fell for women superheroes whose only powers were invisibility or projecting force fields.) That's why when I started hearing the first corridos about the narco or reading the early novels about them, I kept what I liked to call a critical distance. That constructed distance, a distance others confused with fear or caution, collapsed last week when *Proceso* published an interview with Mayo Zambada, a powerful drug lord on the run, conducted by esteemed leftist journalist Julio Scherer García.[2] Suddenly, everybody had an opinion about this rare interview. Suddenly, the news cycle washed us onto the shore of our worst nightmares. What country is this, Agripina?

In what is now understood to have been a well-organized media strategy, Zambada—El Mayo, as he is known—had the good sense to be interviewed by Julio Scherer García. He chose well. He chose the journalist who dedicated hours of his professional life to Sandra Ávila, the cartel leader who will live on in history as La Reina del Pacífico, or the Queen of the Pacific—in part thanks to Scherer's book. El Mayo circumvented younger journalists and those closer to government ranks, and instead opted for this elderly man who, as editor in chief of Mexico's *Excelsior* newspaper between 1968 and 1976, had the nerve to challenge party officials. El Mayo chose Scherer, and he flaunted his choice by posing next to him, standing tall with his chin raised, his right arm circling behind the old man's back. A picture of two comrades in arms. El Mayo chose him, he said, because he had read his work. In a country where the average number of books read in a year is a scandalous one, this declaration does have its evocative relevance.

El Mayo's explicit messages in the interview were, indeed, explicit: he did not plot to kill Felipe Calderón, the army commits atrocities, corruption is what keeps drug trafficking alive, therefore the Mexican war on drugs is lost. To make matters worse, reality immediately validated his claims: the army murdered two boys on the Nuevo Laredo–Matamoros–Reynosa highway on Easter Sunday, just a day before the interview was released. The most important part of the interview was not, however, what was said outright but what was left unsaid. Because if what we want is to prevent the narco from self-mythologizing, or even boasting about itself—a real danger in a country in which a law that is perceived as illegitimate is often opposed by a powerful force of illegality—it is necessary to ground his discourse back in the very terrain of Mexico and its history.

Before making those declarations in the interview, Zambada described himself as a family man. He said: Let's talk first. You don't need to be an expert in hermeneutics or in reading between the lines to catch Zambada's meaning: a discourse where gender roles are not only well-defined but also, and more importantly, unevenly powered. In the interview, Zambada presents himself as a family man, a patriarch aware of and concerned about the fate of his wife, his five children, one of which, the firstborn, he admits "crying over." He also mentions, albeit briefly, his five mistresses, fifteen grandchildren, and one great-grandchild, all, according to him, "gente del monte" (mountain people), just like himself. He does not, of course, speak of the powerful Reinas del Sur, the Queens of the South—women who, like Sandra Ávila, were born within his ranks and thus enjoy certain permissiveness and autonomy. Neither does he allude to the charismatic buchonas, female escorts adept to city life. He does not speak about the decapitated women who appear—at least one in Tijuana, not too long ago—on the highway after what may have been a romantic transgression. To attempt to demystify the narco, we should begin by critiquing the notions of masculinity that it embodies. If Zambada had wanted, astutely, to sketch out his definition of a trustworthy man using phrases such as "you have my word," "my wife, five mistresses, fifteen grandchildren," "my son," "agriculture and livestock," and "they all lie," he should have also remembered that pervasive gender violence in Ciudad Juárez—and in places where the statistics are even more alarming, like in the State of Mexico—is related in large part to aggressive responses to reconfigurations of the nuclear family and shifting gender roles in contemporary Mexico. Carlos Carrera, with a screenplay by Sabina Berman, depicted this perfectly in his 2009 film *El Traspatio* (*Backyard*).

Another way to demystify the drug lord's cavalier image of himself is to question his material and cultural allegiance to our country's most dispossessed classes. Zambada allies himself with the working classes by claiming to be a very specific kind of contemporary peasant: he not only describes himself as a "child of the mountain" but also speaks at length about the earth and sky, with appreciation for the former and distrust for the latter. In fact, toward the end of the interview, he confessed that he made a living working in "agriculture and livestock." But neither Zambada nor Calderón ever mention the obvious: that these agricultural businesses have become major globalized corporations and that, despite the fact that Zambada brushes it off as pure "nonsense," El Chapo's fortune is listed in *Forbes*. The bosses' bosses are far from "gente del monte": thousands of such businessmen conceal their names and the fortunes they have amassed in connection to drug trafficking. They are the post-monte people, and judging by the frenzy, close readers of popular media. They are the narco. Neo-hicks. Wannabe owners of villages now defined as global. It is clear that as long as drug use is not decriminalized—that is, while the bosses' bosses and shadowy businessmen continue to make money off it—then this business will not disappear on its own.

When Zambada explained that he had escaped from the army on several occasions thanks to his knowledge of the land, he also aligned himself, metaphorically and not, with peasant guerrilla traditions that are at the very heart of Mexican history. His criticism of the atrocities committed by the Mexican Army (just as that same army appears to be leaving Ciudad Juárez) is without a doubt meant to forge a sense of empathy with contemporary citizens who are in pain. He avoids mentioning, of course, the atrocities committed by the narco, the ones that have devastated entire rural and urban areas in recent years.

And he was able to avoid mentioning them because, from what can be deduced from the few words he said to Scherer, Zambada continues to think that, unlike the army, the narco only takes revenge or, in any case, uses violence against its equals. And we, those who are increasingly less *we*—thus, self-protected in a pronoun made out of frail wall—know quite well that that isn't true. The massacres of students in Ciudad Juárez and Monterrey are an alarming reminder, among so many others that get lost in the pages of the local press or that hardly make a peep under the incessant murmur, that the honorability of the narco, if it ever did exist, is something of the past. Let us also not forget about the ongoing massacres within a wide range of state institutions. There, in schools or in prisons, lie the twenty-three percent of those executed who are younger than twenty-three years old. We are all vulnerable to the hitmen of today. We are all potential victims.

Subordination is a word full of implications, and many of them, whether explicitly or implicitly, help define Zambada's concept of *pueblo*, or the people, in discourse. And in this, as in his way of culturally and materially aligning himself with various dispossessed classes, Zambada emulates the glory days of the PRI. Remember that the incorporation of workers and peasants into the state apparatus was, from the beginning, highly selective: they let in those who capitulated, like the unions that would later form the powerful confederation, the Confederacíon de Trabajadores de México (CTM; the Confederation of Mexican Workers), but rejected independent workers and anarchists. *Pueblo* and *subordination* both constitute a pleonasm in that lexicon. In all caps the anonymous commenters announced, for example, a curfew, and at the same time, promised familiar protection for "the people" but not for the "people who aren't." Who are these "people who aren't"? The definition follows almost naturally. It is a colloquial phrase, at the end of the cutoff sentence: the people who aren't *with them*. "We are Tamaulipas," they write several times. Insisting. What's true is that people did not leave their homes. What's true is that the "people who aren't" cannot be more numerous than the people who are. What's true is that there is the possibility that they are not, in fact, Tamaulipas.

If to all this we add the imposing, even jovial figure of El Mayo, who placed his right arm around the tired shoulder of the old journalist as he proudly challenged the camera, it is understandable that we, all of us, the *us* in full lowercase, have lost the war that we never even wanted. The equation is easy: people like Zambada, who are attentive to public discourse and popular sentiment, who manipulate notions of masculinity that tie in perfectly with secular machismos, versus people like Calderón, who is incapable of creating even rhetorical bonds with the majority in pain, who is enclosed in his ivory tower from which he only sometimes leaves in order to reprimand the bad behavior of the former, who lacks empathy, who cares more about his abstract legitimacy than his work. How do you compare a man who talks about crying for his son with another who isn't even capable of listening to—not to mention being moved by—a mother who just lost two of her children due to the violence inflicted by that other one who says he cries for his own? Let us not forget Doña Luz María Dávila, of Villas de Salvárcar in Ciudad Juárez, Chihuahua, mother of Marcos and José Luis Piña Dávila, nineteen and seventeen years old. Incapable of embracing the people, and I say this in the broadest sense of the term, both Calderón and his wife understandably disappoint and enrage. Incapable of moving from their seats, of straying from protocol. Since they already had the gall to start a war that we didn't ask for, that we don't support, is it too much to ask that they have the courage to face the consequences of their actions and, if nothing else, to simply blink? At least on the ground, the narco is not only winning the war because of the money they filter to the poor (although the earnings of hitmen apprentices are not as high as one might imagine), they are winning because, as the journalist Gabriela Warkentin argues in an article published in *El País* about the photo of Scherer and Zambada,[3] all of us, truly all of us, saw ourselves in it. Disconcerted, crestfallen, taken by surprise, willing to admit it or not, all of us were there.

XVII

The Neo-Camelias

"In the old days, at least there was some respect for women and children," Don Epifanio Vargas—a narco-turned-politician—says to Teresa Mendoza, the future Reina del Sur, in Spanish author Arturo Pérez-Reverte's famous novel *The Queen of the South*.[1] Those who have read the book will recall that, before she became the businesswoman who established an illegal empire at the mouth of the Mediterranean, Teresa Mendoza was just the girlfriend—not the buchona!—of Güero Dávila, a pilot who was blown up in the middle of a landing strip for trying to outsmart his bosses. Don Epifanio, true to his word, provides Teresa the contacts that will help her escape the narco's revenge, though by then she had already gone through the obligatory rape, reckless car chase, and classic gun-to-the-temple situation found in such novels. It's when Don Epifanio considers helping her that the line *in the old days* falls from his mouth with a heavy note of nostalgia. *In the old days*, he seems to be saying, *things were dealt with between men. In the old days, you got some respect*, he seems to conclude as the logical result, then, for children and women. Something must have changed since.

We can presume that only in those mythical olden days could there have existed a character like Camelia "La Texana"—that woman immortalized in "Contrabando y traición" (Contraband and betrayal), a 1971 corrido by the norteño band Los Tigres del Norte. Now, in 2009, in light of the recent decapitation of Adriana Ruiz Muñiz—an edecán, or brand promoter that markets her sexual appeal, from Tijuana who presumably had ties to narco men—it is difficult to believe the romance between Camelia and Emilio Varela described in the corrido. Emilio and Camelia become lovers as they cross the border between Mexico and the United States with a shipment of "grass." Once they complete their mission, Varela unexpectedly gives his part of the earnings to Camelia, suggesting she rebuild her life as he prepares to return home to his wife, "his true love." Some thirty years later, it's difficult to imagine such a civil breakup between drug traffickers. And, as the lyrics unfold, we realize that such civility was not possible even then. There it is: Emilio Varela invites Camelia to move on with her life, enjoying what he had wanted for himself. And there Camelia is: instead of settling for the feminine decorations of the narco (jewelry, cars, trips), she avenges herself ("Seven shots sounded," the song goes) and keeps the entire shipment she helped carry over the border. The Camelias of today aren't usually like that. Everything seems to indicate that love in the time of drug trafficking has new rules.

A decade after the smash success of this corrido, though still during the good old days that Don Epifanio Vargas longs for, there was also Sara Cosío Vidaurry. Girlfriend (supposedly kidnapped) of Rafael Caro Quintero, one of the most powerful narco bosses during the eighties, she was in his company when he was finally arrested. Described by her father as a "strong-willed" young woman, the daughter of a good family from

Jalisco, she was only a seventeen-year-old high school student when Quintero was arrested in 1985. That Sara Cosío survived the romance—even after testifying against the boss, who went to prison—is yet more proof that the rules of the old days, indeed, might have been different.

The so-called buchonas existed in the good old days and still do exist today. They are the beautiful, uneducated young women who accompany narco men to wild parties or in flashy new cars, wearing loud jewelry and flaunting their enviable bodies. A sort of trophy wife, though without the civil status included. A sort of pigeon that displays an exaggerated volume of chest. A recent example is the sadly famous Miss Sinaloa 2008, Laura Elena Zúñiga Guisar, the young woman who was dating Ángel Orlando García Urquiza, presumed leader of the Juárez cartel, when he was arrested with guns and thousands of dollars on his person. Perhaps in the old days she wouldn't have ended up in jail, but in today's world, she did. Having worked as a model for an agency, Laura Zúñiga had previously spoken out about the profession's low wages (the most she earned for a job done for Pepsi was about forty thousand pesos, when the average remained at two thousand pesos per catwalk), as well as the media's widespread discrimination in favor of foreigners. Similar complaints about the lack of employment and earnings were put forward by Alejandra González Licea, a literature professor at the Universidad Autónoma de Baja California, when she was caught collecting money from the narco in Tijuana. From buchonas to professors, it's clear that the neo-Camelias have diversified.

But the news of Adriana Ruiz Muñiz's brutal murder is something specifically contemporary. The model and edecán for the division-A soccer team Xoloitzcuintles, owned by the Hank family, was presumed to have maintained some sort of "sentimental relationship" (in their words) with Teo's people, or even with Teo himself, the boss of Tijuana's plaza. Executed—tortured and decapitated when she was still alive—Adriana Ruiz's body is perhaps the most obvious example of the changes that have taken place in the relationships between narco men on one hand, and women and children on the other. How far this Baja Californian neo-Camelia was from cursing her Emilio Varela, like in the song! The neo-Camelias are less like the Queen of the South Teresa Mendoza and more like the anonymous women murdered in Ciudad Juárez and other cities in a country at war. They, like Adriana Ruiz, confirm that—in the step from marijuana to cocaine, and later heroin, and with a presidential war in the midst—gender hierarchies are increasingly deadly in the world of the narco.

XVIII

The Longest Sunday

1

Out of everything that day, I remember the dunes. The tremendously blue sky and the clouds, abundant and jumbled, bright white, over the sandy horizon. I remember the footprints left behind by a beetle who so slowly dragged itself over the Samalayuca Dune Fields. A breath of silence, that I remember. Gazing at objects around you for so long yet not understanding. Or understanding, on the contrary, all at once, their magnificent brutality. So this was Ciudad Juárez. From afar, taking refuge in the shadow cast by their pickup, a group of men were drinking beer. Their bodies in a semicircle. The only woman, a young girl with long hair and tight pants, came and went with some of them from the bottom of a dune to the top. Does she not know? I wondered. Is she not afraid? I insisted silently as I watched her smile in the distance. Sand between fingers, falling. Sand, under the weight of a body. And her hair flying away with the wind toward some other place.

2

I remember, I will never forget, her words. I remember Luz María Dávila's words. Just a few days before, in what was still being called a "mistake," a group of hitmen had murdered seventeen youths who had gathered in Villas de Salvárcar, a community in the southwest of Ciudad Juárez, the most dangerous city in Mexico, if not the whole world. Two of those boys were her sons: Marcos and José Luis Piña Dávila, nineteen and seventeen years old, respectively. Her only sons. Los piñitas, that's what she called them. Little pineapples. The news of the massacre, yet another incident in a surge of violence that hasn't slowed since President Felipe Calderón imposed his failed drug war, left very few unafraid. Luz María Dávila, a worker in a maquiladora that made speakers, had uttered words that, being as they were, powerful and trembling, were also simple and accurate: You are not welcome, Señor Presidente. I do not extend my hand to you. Luz María Dávila, a short woman in a blue sweater—that's how the journalist Sandra Rodríguez Nieto described her in *El diario de Juárez*—had said those words in a public forum, next to a president who couldn't even blink.

3

I remember my anxiety before the trip. At that point, Calderón's war had already claimed between fifty and sixty thousand victims, fragmenting families and breaking down the social fabric of Mexico with equal measures of violence and impunity. A somber air was blowing over entire regions of the country, but along with the accumulated news of femicides, Ciudad Juárez continued to occupy a sadly privileged place in our geographies of contemporary horror. Why would anyone go there? I remember its wide streets, empty of people, the string of abandoned houses that lined the road all the way from the airport to the hotel. A black hole in the very heart of the city. An immovable immobility. That way of repeatedly looking over your shoulder like you were expecting the worst, sure it would come at any second. I remember the huizaches on the other side of the car windows, that run-down green. Soft whispering in restaurants, constant warnings, signs prohibiting certain actions, that I remember. News encoded as rumor: Did you know? Did you hear? To you too? I remember all this as life in a time of war.

4

I remember the car photographer Julio Aguilar drove me in, down long, lonely roads under the Sunday sun, to Salvárcar. Its faded seats, broken windows, dubious brakes. I remember his voice, the voice of that man, on our way: *I write with the light.* Giant Greek letters tattooed on his left forearm. I remember the speed we went. Villas de Salvárcar is not at the end of the world but in Ciudad Juárez. It isn't a marginal neighborhood full of makeshift housing or houses without municipal services, but a community with paved streets and cement buildings where Luz María Dávila's family chose to move nine years ago, in search of a better future for her two sons, Marcos and José Luis. The colorful condos. *The Villa S. Union Invites You to Its Third Gran Kermes this October 2 at 5:00 p.m., to benefit the Medical Dispensary.* The rebar pointing toward the sky. Confirmation class. The gray concrete walls. *In memory of Wicho.* With her husband's salary, a security guard in a maquiladora, and the money Luz María Dávila earned as a factory worker, they were slowly remodeling their home. *Martínez Grocery. Thank you for choosing us.* They installed, for example, a built-in, American-style kitchen and converted what had been a bedroom into the living room. *Emergency numbers: 629 33 07 / 629 33 80.* They built more. I remember, among the many magnets that stood out on the refrigerator, colorful fruit, smiling bees, plants with legs and mouths, and that photo of Los Tigres del Norte, all dressed in light blue, promoting their corrido "La Reina del Sur."

5

I remember Luz María Dávila's voice; I remember her shockingly soft voice. Her figure, just as the journalist Sandra Rodríguez Nieto described it, is slight. I have seen the photographs that Julio Aguilar took of her then but, still, it is difficult to recognize her when she opens the door to her home. She is a tiny woman, indeed. Short, curly hair. A hint of gray. I remember that; I remember her way of moving around the furniture and picking up, as if they were fragile antiques, the spoons. And if you didn't know that her only two sons had been gunned down in one of those lethal "mistakes" that abound in cities under narco law, it would be difficult to connect her delicate movements greeting you at the door, her calm way of speaking, all her emotional control, with that of a grieving mother.

I want the guilty ones. As long as no one is found guilty it is as if they were taking away my boys every day. That's what I would say to Señor Presidente today, seven months later. I would tell him that I have faith. That I want to have faith. I have not been disrespectful or rude. I would tell him again that, if they had been his children, if his children were now in a cemetery, he would have turned over every rock. We need to put the three branches of government to work. It is his duty to put an end to this impunity.

6

I remember her voice broke, sometimes, when talking about them, about her sons. I remember how it took her no time at all to compose herself. A tear or two. Nothing that she couldn't wipe away with a napkin or a moment of silence. Her eyes, downcast. Immobile. Then, in the least-expected moment, in the middle of everything, her gaze. An open thing. Her way of blinking.

They were good boys, my boys. Whoever says otherwise is lying. Look at the house where they died. Half a block from here. We had them get together there so they wouldn't go off to other dangerous places. We watched over them from here. I would go halfway into the street from time to time to assure myself, like all of us, that they were okay. That they were not alone. That they were not beyond our reach.

7

I remember the question I kept under my tongue until I reached Salvárcar. Some argue that to repeat the story of violence is to deepen the violence. Some say, in their name, in the name of all the victims, that it is now necessary to start talking about the good parts of Ciudad Juárez. When I ask her what she thinks of that, I also tell her that, in my opinion, her dignity and her bravery are part of the good things we must start talking about.

We have to talk about what is bad because it is bad. Because if we don't, no one is ever going to catch those who are guilty of so many deaths. Things are not good here. They haven't been good here for many years. Now they [the government] are here in the community, building a library, a dispensary, a park. And that's good. But everything else remains the same. Talking about all this isn't just to deepen the wound. It's to change the things that need to be changed. We have to work with the three branches of government. It is the responsibility of the president to put an end to this impunity.

8

I would talk with Señor Presidente's wife. Her people have tried to get in touch with me, but often during the morning, when I'm at work. But I would still talk with her, woman to woman. Mother to mother. She should understand. She could, perhaps, open the president's heart. Make him understand that we cannot continue like this. That it is his responsibility to put an end to impunity. To this. That's what the president is for. I have faith. I want to have faith.

9

I remember the car headlights on Ciudad Juárez's nocturnal streets. I remember, in that moment, right there, the way Sandra Rodríguez shifted gears in her car. Someone is following us, I remember her saying at one point while looking in her rearview mirror. To accelerate is a violent action. Do you see that empty lot? There used to be a building there. Do you see that hole in the wall? That happened just a month ago. Do you see that corner? They killed a friend of mine there. The city like a trail of crosses. That kind of city you must traverse to reach one of the few bars that are still open downtown. I remembered the phrase "to finish off a beer" as we finished off a couple of beers and played songs by Lucha Reyes and Bob Dylan on an old jukebox. I remember her conclusion, as basic and brutal as Luz María Dávila's words: impunity as the source of evil. There are now at least two generations of boys growing up in an atmosphere where it is "natural" to witness the massive death of women, of young men, of everyone. There are now two or three generations of children who grew up with mothers leaving early for work and returning, if they do return, late at night. Who haven't experienced a mother's care. A mother's recognition. While they know that any action can go unpunished, things will never change. I remember these words from Sandra Rodríguez Nieto.

10

I am not a journalist, I remember saying at the beginning of our conversation. What I want is to get to know you, to speak with you. And she, who just a few days ago hosted Italian and Spanish journalists—people who, according to her, can report on everything they see and hear because they don't have to live here—has opened the doors to her home, apologizing because she could only offer us a few tamales and water for Nescafé. I remember the wax figurines sitting on napkins embroidered with stitched crosses. I remember the key ring on the living room wall. The umbrella hanging from the refrigerator handle, that I remember too. I am not a journalist, I remember repeating to her as an excuse when she brought out photographs of her boys and placed them on the table and I couldn't help but burst into tears. He could be my son, I remember thinking.

They are the faces of so many boys and adolescents and teenagers I see every day on the street, in classrooms. That Luz María Dávila's pain even allows her to console me, offering me a napkin and her open gaze and her hand, that same hand that she did not want to and could not offer the president, forces me to compose myself.

I remember my shame.

I remember how I started to breathe again.

11

I remember the steps—few, unsteady, trembling—inside the house of the massacre. I remember the traces of blood on the walls: hands. They are children's hands. Boys' hands. Human hands. Do I remember that? On the way back, when we had already passed by the security personnel that still safeguard the house, by the paintings commemorating some of the fallen, by the new library whose walls are decorated with children's colorful handprints, I ask Julio Aguilar how he does it. How do you survive in this city taking photos of ten to fourteen bodies a day? I remember his laughter. Julio, indeed, laughs. I write with the light, he says. As the day goes by I become warped, but sometimes, when something about the landscape is able to move me—a cloud, a plant, the rain—I see that I am still human. Then I am sure that I will survive. I am going to die doing this, you know? It isn't for the money. It's because I write with the light. That's how.

12

I remember that, as we traveled down the wide and lonely streets of Ciudad Juárez, as we passed those holes that violence and impunity were opening in the urban fabric of the city, I wondered about the hours of her Sunday. Luz María Dávila's Sunday. I remember the word *zozobra*, or anxiety. I remember I read it for the first time years ago in a Russian novel, and because I didn't know what it meant, I looked it up in the dictionary: From the lat. *sub*, below, and *supra*, above. 4. Intr. *To be restless and uneasy because of insecurity about something or the uncertainty about what should be done.* I remember I pictured her flowers, all the paper flowers that she now makes, the way she passes the time that she no can longer enjoy with her sons. The word *zozobra* is a feminine noun. It means restless, affliction, and distress of the spirit that does not settle or of the risk that threatens, or of the illness that is already being suffered. I remember having pictured her repeating in silence the words she said to me out loud: I have faith. I want to have faith. Señor Presidente, it is your responsibility.

13

I remember the overwhelmingly blue sky. The sky that was a sky in excess. I remember the dunes, and on the dunes, the colorful paper flowers, and around the flowers, the hands of a long, very long Sunday, and around that Sunday, a slow beetle continues to drag itself over the sandstone of Ciudad Juárez.

XIX

A Network of Holes

They left Ciudad Victoria at four in the morning in order to reach Zacatecas by noon. It was 2010, and we wanted to take advantage of my participation in a literary festival there. We found that surprising, mythical midpoint on the map—a colonial city for which we shared a mutual love—and finally made a many-times-postponed gathering happen. You have to accept it: there always comes that moment in life when neither Facebook nor Twitter nor Messenger is enough to satisfy the desire to meet in person. That old babit. It gave me pleasure to see my friends arrive, wide awake and somewhat frenzied. It gave me pleasure to hug them and to begin, around a table, the conversation that has brought us together since the first time we met, years ago, there in the shared land of our birth: Tamaulipas. It took very little time for Claudia Sorais Castañeda to acknowledge it: They came to Zacatecas scared to death. Scared shitless. Both Marco Antonio Huerta and Sara Uribe, poets that reside in the port of Tampico, admitted it immediately too: they were also scared. None of them had had the heart to admit it in the car that Claudia drove under the norteño sky, but every mile they traveled forced them to stay vigilant and quiet. Light conversation. A forced smile. Every-thing else causing alarm. Not long ago, on those very roads, though a little farther north, the army had massacred the boys Martín and Bryan Almanza Salazar, an act that has still gone unpunished today. For example. On those very roads, also not long ago, they murdered a candidate for governor. On those very roads, just a few days ago, though farther to the east, the bodies of seventy-two migrants massacred by the narco were found. Our conversation in Zacatecas could not avoid the facts. Are things really as bad as the newspapers say they are? I asked, referring to the intimate atmosphere of their neighbor-hoods or families. When they turned their heads and lowered their voices to respond, I learned that things were even worse.

The Lawless Roads is the title of a book by Graham Greene. It alludes to Mexico.

But these roads of Tamaulipas were the very roads of my childhood. And I want them back. We drove on them at dawn or in broad daylight, from Matamoros to Tampico, passing inevitably through San Fernando to visit friends or family. How many times did we leave Matamoros very early in the morn-ing to go to Reynosa and from there to cross to McAllen? On the highways and then through the openings between ejidos, we would also drive to the miniscule Santa Rosalía cemetery, where the bones of our eldest ancestors rest. We would travel from Tampico to Mante to visit an aunt in the middle of sum-mer: If that isn't hell, then what is? I remember the afternoon that we were sitting in the bed of a pickup—the wind in my face, the faint light of the first stars—right before reaching San Fernando to get gas. The ferry crossing from Tuxpan to Tam-pico. The lines of cars or people on the bridge that connects Matamoros to Brownsville. They are not the lawless roads that Greene describes; the roads belong to my family and to the families like my family. They're mine. They're ours. And as I said: I want them back.

I just retweeted Elda Cantú, border resident between Nuevo León and Tamaulipas: "In twenty years we will talk about 2010: At night there were gunshots and by day we went to work. On the roads, blockades. It will be a bad memory."

I could not answer a message Claudia Sorais wrote from Ciudad Victoria, Tamaulipas: "Virtual hugs from this north that is hurting."

I've already read "Is This a Party?"—the article in which Sara Uribe questions, from Tamaulipas, the commemoration of the bicentennial.

This is where we are: a fatally failed war against the narco. This is what we are dealing with: a characteristically indifferent response from the president when confronted with the massacre of seventy-two migrants.

Because of this and more I was tempted to join the active mourning initiative launched on Facebook. The action has been simple but powerful: it has involved replacing one's profile picture with a black square. The result at first glance is dramatic. As the number of participants increased, my feed became a collection of black holes. Looking at them, I couldn't help but wonder, with the words that the defeated used before a Mexico City already taken by the enemy: Will our inheritance be a network of holes?

Another way of asking the same question is: Will they steal the others' roads to the future just like they stole those of my childhood?

I respect and share the indignation that inspired this active mourning initiative online. Unlike the cynics and nihilists, I still believe that these kinds of actions produce what we most need today: A sense and a practice of community. A recognition in others. Nevertheless, I resisted cutting my face out of the picture because I believe that erasing your face under a blanket of darkness is precisely what creates violence. The murderer kills before tightening the noose or administering the coup de grace; the murderer kills after they cover their victim's face with a sheet of silence or indifference. Against the fainthearted who never show their face or the corrupt who avoid facing the consequences of their actions, I prefer to expose my face. Because, as the French philosopher Levinas said: The face demands. The face claims. The face, by the mere fact of existing, requires a response: this: the presence. And Peter Sloterdijk writes it in his first volume of *Spheres*: "The opening up of the face—even more than cerebralization and the creation of the hand—enabled people to become animals open to the world, or, more significantly, to their fellow humans."[1] This is where we stand: Better to show your face and force the guilty to face the facts. Better to open ourselves to others' faces, to recognize their humanity. Honor it. The face is a door. The face connects, inevitably. An out-ward motion: the face. A toward-you. Look at me, you tell us.

XX

Under the Glare with Guillermo Fernández

March 2012 marked the highest number of murders in ten months. According to *Milenio*'s count, the "total executions so far in the six-year term increases to 50,093, 3,138 of which took place during the first third of 2012." In what was qualified as a "significant upturn of violence," there was an average of 36.8 deaths a day during the month of March. One of the victims, whose killing occurred on the last day of the month, was Guillermo Fernández, a Tapatío poet and translator who had lived in Toluca, the highest city in Mexico, for some twenty years. Though the conditions of his death are still not entirely clear, the brief journalistic notes on the subject stress the violence of the crime perpetrated at night, inside his own home. The adjective and the noun: brown packing tape. The noun and the verb: hands tied. The final point: a blow to the head. How many times have we read descriptions like this? I detest writing about recently deceased friends or teachers, above all because writing about one obliges me to write about all, but on this occasion I do it to add my voice to those of so many writers and friends who, from Mexico City and the surrounding state as well as other regions of the country, have demanded the prompt clarification of facts and the impartation of justice. I also do not want this crime, yet another crime, to go unpunished. I also do not want Guillermo Fernández, or anyone else, to become one more horrific statistic in a country that is falling to pieces. Isn't that true, Agripina? I also ask for justice.

It is so difficult to write this.

I was not a good friend of Guillermo Fernández, not even close, but as a sporadic resident of that highland city, I did have the privilege of occasionally sharing time with him. Like many living in the capital of a state that has paid little attention to its cultural life, I attended, on several occasions, both the poetry and translation workshops that he led in the Casa de la Cultura like someone who has found a little fresh air in a stuffy crowd. Those who know how stifling life can be in certain industrial cities of the Mexican province should easily be able to picture the aura of ultimate refuge and the festive tone that these meetings would acquire. Always maintaining—and in spite of the years—his perspective as a newcomer there, Guillermo Fernández contributed to maintaining and expanding a cultural environment often dull and more often tied up due to lack of resources or internal conflicts. His irony, his integrity and autonomy, and above all, his tireless work, encouraged young, rebellious men and women to immerse themselves in the dark corners of poetry.

Indeed, Guillermo Fernández was a passionate and devoted translator from the Italian. Like anyone else who has read Italo Calvino or Eros Alessi in Spanish, I also owe much to his constant, disciplined, careful, poorly paid labor. But I owe him more. My love for Xinantécatl, or Nevado de Toluca, which I insisted on visiting at least once a year for a long time, is something I developed thanks to the long journeys that Guillermo organized to listen, on one of the peaks of the world, to his favorite music. Opera. It was from him that I inherited the sacred habit of adding cardamom to coffee beans. And there was quite a lot of music that I discovered or rediscovered thanks to him, but among all of them I remember delicious hours discussing the voice of Lucha Reyes in detail, especially her way of enunciating the lines of "La mensa"—her song in which a woman *wilts, wilts, wilts*. Once in a talk on politics, he arrived at the exact definition of power: power is not being able to go out onto the street. I remember immediately tweeting that maxim. He and I got on each other's nerves quite easily, but to be honest, we never stopped talking during those meetings in the highlands. Once he came to my house in Metepec without an invitation, something he rarely did, and he sat at the table (at a corner) and started to talk about his life. More than on any other occasion, the Guillermo in front of me was not the (almost) eighty-year-old man but instead four twenty-year-old youths put together, all in one. I never learned what was and was not true in that story that I am now confusing with the glare of the afternoon: the boy who escapes from his house at nine years old, the young man who meets Eugenio Montale in person, the older man who continuously discovers that, above everything, he prefers solitude and poetry. Between one thing and another I brought out a bottle of tequila—as far as I know, his favorite drink. And I listened to him. It must have been Saturday or Sunday. I never learned why he did that; what prompted him to knock on my door and then to stay. That marvelous and clear afternoon, that afternoon that surely was a spring Saturday, is entirely whole now, here.

Standing in the memory of that afternoon, under its relentless glare, I demand, as many others do, that the state clarify the facts and that justice be served.

These are but a few lines, maestrín.

XXI

Under the Narco Sky

I had good friends in my early twenties. I knew it then, when life was all about rummaging through the world and going for radical extremes, but I know it even more now, when I find myself citing their words left and right. With a pen in his left hand and staring off behind some giant cloud, one of those unforgettable friends once said, "It's not strange that it doesn't exist, but that it *does* exist, you know?" He was talking about love, of course, a phenomenon against which we were writing a long, furious manifesto. The idea had formed, like most things did back then, at the root of some clever joke. In those days, we were completely against romance. The way new lovers displayed their affections made us fall into a kind of frenzied depression. The resigned domestic attitude of men and women who had been, until recently, perfectly independent and autonomous, plunged us into lengthy metaphysical trances. The tiresome repetition of loving gestures and words drove us to parody it, and from there, between fits of laughter, to the writing of that manifesto, still unpublished. The notion that it's incredible that this thing keeps existing materialized during one of those rare moments I would label as epiphanic. Indeed, even when our criticism of love was precise and urgent and vitriolic, we had enough self-awareness to bow down and accept the inacceptable. Delighted. That phrase we articulated came to mind not long ago, while I was reading reports on the narco's bloody practices along the northern border. A day before, I had crossed the border into Tijuana, interning myself yet again in what the newspapers call El Teo's (alias "El Tres Letras") plaza. I remembered that my friends don't go out as much as they used to, preferring to hang out in people's homes to avoid shoot-outs as much as possible. I also recalled the many stories about the kidnapping of a cousin or grandchild or parent and I envisioned their preoccupied eyes, upright fists, drawn faces. I slowed down, as I was signaled to do, as I approached a military checkpoint that five years ago, when I first left this border city, didn't yet exist on this road that I use to get home. I slowed down again when a convoy of four police trucks passed by on my right at top speed: sirens on, lights flashing red. So this is what it's like to live in the narco empire? I asked myself, but my question was more of a confirmation, a verification. So this is what it's like to live in a state of siege? So this is the war?

When I finally got to their house, we were careful to lock all the doors. In suspiciously low voices, as if we feared the retaliation of ghosts, we started in on typical norteña chitchat: a friend of a friend's disappearance; the gruesome details that make the kidnappers' lives all the more interesting—their lack of empathy, their boundless cruelty, their manner of work; the fear that causes a neighbor to lean out their window to look for something and that also encourages them to shut the curtains tight afterward; the corruption of a police force that is clearly at the service of the narco, not the state; the corruption of politicians. The death that, in effect, reigns supreme. It was then that my friend's epiphanic phrase on love from so many years ago sprung to mind, though somewhat distorted (now we elite scholars would say something like "intervened upon," but it's all the same). After thousands and thousands of deaths, after so many days living in the turmoil of a country run amok by war since 2006, it's not strange that there doesn't exist an organized civil society ready to check an inept, clumsy governing class, but that it *does* still exist. It's not at all strange that a good portion of clearheaded Mexicans decided to cast a null vote, but that others, the rest of us, continue to bet on democracy purely by showing up to the polls. It's not unusual that fear paralyzes us but that, sometimes, it also provokes a desire to speak, and to speak up. It's not strange that cruelty exists here among us; what's strange is that, with the number of femicides increasing in this region and all over the country, sometimes, it seems a bit less present.

I thought of the phrase again when I saw a man and a woman holding hands at the taqueria where I was having breakfast. They weren't young, but there, with their damp hair, smiling absentmindedly at each other as they entered, they seemed ageless. It was clear that they were lovers. Moreover, that they were in love. Even as they sat across the wooden table from each other, their bodies were still attuned to an atmosphere shared by no one else. A delicate soap bubble around them. A membrane as light as worn silk. They ordered a simple breakfast, and while they ate their food, they spoke in the lowered tone that betrays shared intimacy. An old-fashioned courtesy between them. Thank you, they said. Please. If my friends and I had seen them back then, when we'd first had the idea to draft our manifesto against love, surely we would have written something else entirely. But what is strange, I thought at that moment, is not that rage and death, corruption and cruelty, multiply and grow under the narco sky, but that these two lovers exist, here, recently showered, lavishing on each other with the always unprecedented, always unrepeatable, always transparent gestures of something that, if I were a little braver, I would not hesitate to call, fair and square, love.

Writing as We Grieve, Grieving as We Write

XXII

Mourning

I wrote the following piece in 2004.[1] I reproduce it in its entirety now because it is what I will carry under my arm tomorrow, Wednesday, April 6, 2011, when, wherever I am, I will be walking in spirit alongside so many others in the National Emergency March in Mexico City, setting out from the Palacio de Bellas Artes toward the Zócalo in solidarity with our forty thousand dead. I reproduce this piece in its entirety because I do not know any other way to offer my condolences to the poet Javier Sicilia for the death of his son, Juan Francisco, or to the other fathers and mothers who have also been amputated—as the poet fittingly described it—of a child. I reproduce this piece because yes, it's true, just as Sicilia wrote in the open letter that he published in *Proceso* last Sunday, we are fed up.[2] And I reproduce it, too, because, nevertheless, we keep going. And here we keep going.

*

In "Violence, Mourning, Politics," an essay in Judith Butler's *Precarious Life: The Powers of Mourning and Violence*, Butler explores—with the intelligence we have come to know her for, with the political preoccupation and philosophical rigor typical of her—the functions of mourning in a world pierced by sharp, massive manifestations of increasing violence.[3] The event that triggers Butler's concern is not only 9/11 but the political manipulation, especially of the Bushian style, that has sought to transform rage and pain—that is, public and international mourning—into an endless war against the permanently dehumanized Other. That is where Butler begins this essay. She also finishes it there, with a reflection on the human who, in these pages but also outside of them, is transformed into a question that, when summarized, becomes enigmatic: What makes for a grievable life? The answer, of course, is not simple. Moreover, the response invites, in fact obliges, the intersection and contrasting—whichever happens first—of the most intimate and thus the most political aspects of our lives.

To understand the dynamic of mourning, Butler proposes first considering the central dependency that binds the *I* and the *you*. More than relational—a term that, though adequate and common, seems quite aseptic in this case—Butler describes those bonds of dependency, those human relations, as relations of dispossession, that is, relations that are based on more than a tacit understanding of Levinas as the "ways in which we are, from the start and by virtue of being a bodily being, already given over, beyond ourselves, implicated in lives that are not our own."[4] That is how vulnerability constitutes the most basic and even the most radical of the truly human conditions. It is thus urgent to not only recognize that vulnerability at every turn but also to protect it and, furthermore, to preserve it. To perpetuate it. Only in the state of vulnerability, in recognizing the different ways the Other dispossesses me, inviting me to unknow myself, can we understand that the

I was never a beginning nor was it even a possibility. In the beginning there was the *we*, Butler seems to say—*we* being the most intimate and also the most political form of accessing one's subjectivity.

Mourning, the psychological and social process through which the loss of another is publicly and privately recognized, is perhaps the most obvious instance of our vulnerability and, thus, our human condition. When we mourn the death of another, we accept from the outset, whether consciously or unconsciously, that the loss will change us, forever and in definitive ways. "Perhaps mourning has to do with agreeing to undergo a transformation," Judith Butler writes, "the full result of which one cannot know in advance." Because if the *I* and the *you* are connected by those relations of dispossession, with the loss of the Other, one is also confronted with the reality that "something is hiding in the loss, something is lost within the recesses of loss."[5] Grief, then, perhaps like desire, "contains the possibility of apprehending a mode of dispossession that is fundamental to who I am."[6] It follows that by losing the Other, "I not only mourn the loss, but I become inscrutable to myself."[7] The virtue of mourning consists in positioning the *I* neither as an affirmation nor as a possibility but as a way of unknowing. A becoming.

Butler maintains, or makes me believe, that recognizing these basic forms of vulnerability and unknowingness constitutes a foundation, fundamentally ethical, from which to rethink a theory of collective power and responsibility. When not just a few lives are dignified to be publicly grievable, when the obituary covers the nameless and the faceless, when, like Antigone, we are capable of burying the Other, or that which is the same, of recognizing the life lived by that Other, even in spite of and against Creon's edict—or that of any other authority in power—then public mourning, making us more vulnerable, will make us more human. This type of theoretical framework, she says, could help us not respond violently to the harm that others inflict on us, limiting, at the same time, the always latent possibility of the harm that we cause.

Better known for her revelatory arguments about gender identities as unstable and performative conditions, Judith Butler explores in this book the possibility of an ethics of nonviolence that is neither new age nor principled nor rigid. Personal, intimate, passionate, and at the same time rigorous and austere in her arguments, Judith Butler has written one of the most empathetic and intelligent books about pain and justice in the contemporary world.

And I end now as Butler ends one of her essays, writing, "You are what I gain through this disorientation and loss. This is how the human comes into being, again and again, as that which we have yet to know."[8]

XXIII

Writing in Migration: A Desedimentation
with Lina Meruane

The Sound from the Outside

From the beginning, Lina Meruane was, above all, a voice. Or rather: a rhythm. As much in *Seeing Red*, the first novel of hers that I read, as in our first conversation together—on a rainy afternoon in New York, if I remember correctly—what was left etched in my memory most was the cadence of her words. The way her words not only meant something but were something in and of themselves: sound, presence, company. A materiality of echoes. Reverberation. Time has passed and still, when we meet here or there, I continue to be impressed by the contrast between the soft accent, almost singsongy, of her Chilean Spanish, and the lively melody, more noticeable, that pulls it from her lips and deposits it, swiftly, into the air we breathe. It has taken me some time to realize that that contrast of registers and tones is less a result of simple, organic chance and more of the long journey of the "porous languages" that her migrant ancestors learned and practiced throughout their lives. The languages, body movements, and even physical appearances of entire generations are lost, frequently forever, with changes in context, processes of social mobility, and pressure from pop culture, as Annie Ernaux argues in her book *The Years*.[1] But it is also true that, beneath all of that, beyond the mere surface, something sediments in the body. Like trauma that is inherited from generation to generation, the materiality of the experience cuts grooves into the throat, imposes a certain lightness in the hands, is carried in particular ways on the hips. We say: You look so much like your grandmother, without being able to define exactly where that similarity resides. We say: That reminds me of the way your aunt danced, trying to capture an unrepeatable movement. We say: That's a word your grandfather used, awestruck by this unexpected exclamation. Those things that appear or reappear in moments of great stress or much happiness have no calendar or planner. When something is about to break, there they are. When there is nothing more, there they are. During a distraction, in the midst of surrendering, while we laugh or are overcome by a panic attack—above all, in the present. That subterfuge that brings us to our own, making us, in fact, ourselves over time and space is what I heard in Lina Meruane's words. It has taken me time to distinguish in her voice, then, the accents that, even in an apparent immobility, continue moving around. It is the sound from the outside. It has to do with that mark that we carry, whether we know it or not, those of us who are always going somewhere else.

Porous Languages

In *Volverse Palestina* (Becoming Palestinian), in which Lina Meruane explores with loving care the migratory voyage that her grandparents made from Palestine to Chile in the middle of the twentieth century, and in which she also embarks on a return to a place she has never before been all these years later, she pauses for a moment on what she calls "tongues in bifurcation."[2] There are her grandparents, learning, conserving, hiding languages, selecting with mathematical precision the speech that would guarantee a citizenry that wasn't "second class" for their progeny. Arabic. Spanish. German. Even though the information alone is only as reliable as the memory of her family members, it seems clear that her grandmother learned Spanish as a girl upon arriving in the Americas, while her grandfather began to surmount the Castilian vowels when he was already a young man of thirteen or fourteen years, without also discounting all the German that came from the lessons at the religious European community schools that were in operation at that time. More than a disappearance of maternal languages, this has to do with layers of speech that, by accumulating one on top of the other, far from erasing the previous ones, emphasize them with their own existence. There is something beneath the voice, something ineluctable that, nevertheless, may go unnoticed. But not for those who have experienced the outside. Sedimenting with each other, these porous languages open secret tunnels that, in their solidity, allow the free passage of individual inflections, peculiar lilts, modulations that no one who isn't us could ever repeat. How many languages are hidden and how many allow their echoes to be glimpsed in the words we pronounce? Those of us who are products of long migration sagas might not know the answer, but we never stop asking the question.

Desedimenting Language

My paternal grandparents, like Lina Meruane's, left behind a land they would never return to. At the beginning of the twentieth century, they turned their backs on their corner of San Luis Potosí after the endemic dryness of the plateau had snatched their first son. They went north. And once there, they went even farther north. On the border between Coahuila and Texas, they became workers in the coal mines, and later, with a little luck, day laborers on the cattle ranches. Like many dispossessed during the Porfiriato era of the late nineteenth and early twentieth centuries, my grandparents brought very little with them when they left beyond their arms and tongue. They spoke Spanish, that's true. But they also spoke something else. Another tongue, the one they stopped using and that their children did not inherit, the one that will always be a matter of speculation. During the same period, my maternal grandparents crossed the border between Mexico and the United States, becoming cotton pickers and construction workers in huge Texan cities. To the Spanish they carried with them, they soon added English. And some thirty years after their arrival, when President Hoover initiated an aggressive deportation policy following the Great Depression of 1929, my grandparents and their tongues returned to Mexico. There they carved out a life that extended to their children and grandchildren. They stopped talking about their expulsion so as to start talking about their welcoming. I learned little to nothing about those journeys, agreements, humiliations, meetings. In any case, Spanish settled into their bodies and, there, in their lungs and throat, in their larynx, in their torrent of blood, it built its home. Just like Lina Meruane, who returned to Palestine without having been there before, in 1990 I returned to Texas when I believed I was arriving for the first time. My grandparents, who had worked tirelessly there, establishing through marriage the beginning of their family, created the footprint that, as José Revueltas would say, my return inhabited. Recognizing is different from knowing, but they are so similar. Now, after more than thirty years living in the United States, I am sometimes asked about my accent. And these are acquaintances and friends from both the United States and Mexico who ask me. There is, of course, the backbone of Spanish, but at its side, in porous layers, also stretch those other languages that the migrations placed and blurred along the way. That which refuses to die, that rhythm I do not control and notice even less, is the genetic charge of sound in migration.

A Tradition of Long Walks

"The ships set sail from Haifa," says Meruane, "and were docked in some Mediterranean port (Genoa or Marseille) before continuing on to America with their third-class steerages full of Arabs, rats, and hungry cockroaches." She says, too, that those Arabs were Orthodox Christians who were leaving their lands carrying Ottoman passports. They were fleeing from military service, which is the same as saying they were fleeing from the war where they would be "cannon fodder." They were fleeing because staying was an impossibility. A risk. A penitence. My paternal grandparents did the same thing: they escaped from the hunger that years of draught caused; they fled the dispossession of lands that president Porfirio Díaz's policies caused; they left behind that radical poverty in which a stomach disease like dysentery was a death sentence. Revueltas writes in *Human Mourning*, his novel about the Mexican North, that the poor looking for their own place on earth have no other option than to walk fervently. To walk as if life depended on it. Even though the train tracks that united San Luis Potosí with the border had stretched out since the end of the nineteenth century, I believe my grandparents, who didn't have two pennies to rub together, walked the entire route north. It was, as Revueltas writes, "absolutely essential that they keep walking, now that they had no place. That they keep walking intensely

... in search of themselves, because even though they might be defeated something deep inside was whispering to them that salvation existed."[3] Gloria Anzaldúa, another inhabitant of the border between Texas and Tamaulipas, does not stop reminding us, either, that there is, among us, a "tradition of migration, a tradition of long walks."[4]

To Turn Back, Which Is Another Way of Going Toward the Future

It was an afternoon in Chile when Lina Meruane proposed to her father that they begin to "go back, slowly." She wanted to return to her father's city and to his old house, as she puts it, "for us to mend our memory." Not only had her father left Beit Jala behind as a young man but she herself had left Chile years ago to live in the United States. Could it be true that those who move frequently remember more? Melancholy can play mean tricks, without a doubt. Nostalgia. For those who are themselves part of a long lineage of migrations, what remains? In *Volverse Palestina* the list is long: a chicken coop, the sound of a faucet running, a patio with orange trees, a black piano, an umbrella stand, a couple of trees pulling up the asphalt, a main square with its bronze fountain, stores with signs bearing Palestinian last names, the heavy yardstick that was used to measure pieces of fabric, the scissors, the frayed ends, the counter. I close the book for a moment and, staring at the white wall, I turn back: the worn wooden floors, the aroma of quince, the rusted tractors, the mesquite pods, the drains, a rope tied to a branch hanging over a canal, a cast-iron skillet, the sound of the stick on the flour bollos, the organ pipe cacti, the clear-blue sky, the flight of the owl, the air of the first hurricane. These are my memories from Poblado Anáhuac, that place on the border between Tamaulipas and Texas where my parents met and, after marrying and bringing me into the world, left behind. Where are you from? people asked me when I first arrived in a new city. And how do I tell them I had been born in a place that does not appear on maps.

Going with the Body

Slowly, in *Volverse Palestina*, Lina's father takes part in sharing that retrospective movement of memory, but not without reticence. It will require, later, the memory support of aunts, cousins, and even taxi drivers. But eventually, Lina will go for herself. Backward. Toward the future. Her body, which crosses airports, which answers impossible questions, both doubting and raising doubt, goes. Who's who in that world over there, in that injured place that is Palestine—taken, invaded, sliced by walls and violence? And who are we here, so close to those cages where the children who come on foot from Central America are still locked up? Who are we when a lawyer argues before a judge that denying soap to an "illegal" migrant is *not* a violation of human rights? I have already spent months returning to that border strip. As there is no house to return to, I want to at least walk along the paths on which their feet stepped. There is nothing left of my paternal grandparents: a few photographs, two or three rumors, the name of a town. But the journey continues. Their way of migrating, which was their mode of survival, remains. That's why one day at the end of the summer we go to Zaragoza, a village that, until I arrived, I had imagined to be dry and lost, but that ends up being surrounded by springs and tall trees with immense foliage. Zaragoza, Coahuila, an hour from Piedras Negras, crossing the border through Eagle Pass. Cotton fields here and there. After eating and resting, after asking at the police station and later at the town hall offices, we are able to find the local cemetery. Their names do not appear in the books. And all that I manage to learn is that, between tombs, perhaps in the bordering area, there is a mass grave where those who did not have the resources to obtain a piece of land, a coffin, a marble slab, or a cross are laid to rest. There, in that place that I cannot locate, but over which my feet have already tread, are the bones of one of my grandmothers. Her body under my body. My body here, next to hers. I cannot ask for more, nor get less. A closeness that, like the closeness Lina Meruane feels when she is about to leave Palestine, only means that you will return again.

Writing from the United States

There is always someone who has migrated before. That is what I'm trying to say. When we believe we have embarked on this journey with no return, this displacement that subdivides or multiplies into many more, in reality we are fitting the soles of our feet into the footsteps that others have left behind. There is no tabula rasa. We are just guests on the surface of a land that we experience in common. Someone was here, where I am; and someone else will be here after my stay. Someone spoke this language, a language that was denied again and again. The reasons for that absence are the very thing of politics; the reasons for the presence are the very thing of ethics. Between them and us, in any case, there is a bridge that has a strong memory because it is organic and material. Because it affects us and we affect it. Those who write from the United States do not have the luxury of forgetting that we continue to write in migration.

XXIV

Writing against War

There are quite a few horrific, violent scenes in *Safe Area Goražde*, the 2000 journalistic comic book by Joe Sacco about the war in eastern Bosnia, and specifically in Goražde, a small village nestled in the Drina Valley with a predominantly Muslim and Serbian population. In his critical recounting of the pivotal period between 1992 and 1995, scenes in the book depict hunger and growing desperation, the nocturnal shootings that would soon become diurnal too, and later, constant. There are the bloodied waters of a river, the Drina, whose name would later become the name of the cigarettes that eased nerves and served as currency there. At times narrated from the perspective of eyewitnesses and survivors, the shameful Foča and Srebrenica massacres pass through these paneled pages, filled with equal parts illustration and text. The mass rape of women, the mutilated bodies of men and children, the hospitals where surgery was conducted without anesthesia if it could even be done: all of it is in this book.

Perhaps the most chilling aspect of these war-ravaged pages is when the characters, run-of-the-mill inhabitants of Goražde, begin to speak about—at first more in shock than with rage, paralyzed by the kind of horror that often leads to disbelief rather than the desire for revenge—how they came to recognize their neighbors' faces on the bodies of their attackers. And I say that perhaps this is so chilling, because it is there, in that cruel recognition, that the readers of this marvelous, horrific, human, and brutal book finally realize what it means to live during war, to make war, to suffer from it on a daily basis.

In the chapter titled "Neighbors," the mother of Edin, the friend-informant who is the Virgil in charge of guiding both Joe Sacco and us, his readers, through the intricate paths of Goražde during these difficult years, begins to mention the names of their Serbian neighbors in a home movie. The mother recalls, in panels that privilege a face crisscrossed with wrinkles, how they used to drink coffee in their homes or how they celebrated their orthodox Christmases or even how they attended their weddings. "When the Serbs got as close as 50 meters," admits another as he peeks behind a gate and recognizes from afar a soldier in a doorway, "I recognized my neighbors. One of them had spent a lot of time with my youngest son, a lot of time at my house . . . doing homework with my son."[1]

Christopher Hitchens carefully explains in the book's introduction that the horrifying thing about fascism "is that it 'takes' only a few gestures . . . to unsettle or even undo the communal and human work of generations." And he adds that fascists are only brave enough to try it with the "reassurance of support from superiors or aid from an outside power and the need to know that 'law,' defined nationally or internationally, will be a joke at the expense of their victims."[2] According to Hitchens, these three indulgences were granted in Bosnia during the years of the monumental conflict. That's how people forgot their neighbors and shut themselves off in their terror.

That's also how state representatives, originally elected to serve and safeguard the well-being of citizens, chose a nationalist uproar instead of governing, enunciated in this context in ethnic terms to demonstrate that their choice not to govern was correct. That is how the neighborhood or, more generally, the community work of entire generations dissolved into a river (and this is not a metaphor) of blood and impunity.

If some readers believe I am mistaken and, instead of writing about Goražde at the end of the twentieth century I am writing about Mexico at the beginning of the twenty-first, they wouldn't necessarily be wrong. The story that Joe Sacco develops in well-informed passages, through verisimilar and delirious dialogue (perhaps verisimilar because it is so delirious), and with precise and evocative illustrations is, indeed, about the war in eastern Bosnia, but it is above all, and thus inviting parallels with Mexico, about War. It is difficult not to associate the hunger for power, the cynicism and ineptitude of governing institutions, the prevailing rein of corruption and impunity, with the current reality of the country I was born in. The warnings to not drive on the highway are not gratuitous nor are the suggestions, predominantly in certain northern cities, to not go out to dinner much less to go out dancing or enjoy oneself. The things our family members tell us in hushed whispers when they visit us from those border cities are not exaggerations: you can now go to certain areas and the stench of scorched bodies from the ground underneath you isn't so obvious, but things haven't calmed down. It is not an excess of care nor a proclivity for melodrama that makes each farewell be preceded by a "take good care of yourself." No one is sure whether this embrace, the embrace of a goodbye, will be the last.

How many still remember what happened in Bosnia? How

many are still shaken by the name Srebrenica? My fear is that, without a record of testimonials from Mexico's misnamed drug war, without a large community archive that protects victims' voices, we will not only forget the massacres and the pain in years to come but also, and perhaps above all, the labor taken on by entire generations—that amorous and routine, dialogic and constant labor—to form the community that we call a neighborhood. Writing is also a shuddering. And it is our own.

XXV

The End of Women's Silence

A Crónica from a Possible Future

In the future, we will remember those final days of March 2019 as days that made our worlds tremble. We were full of pain and rage, we will say. We were also full of hope. We were, in those days, a furious invocation for the truth. Our voices pierced the air and fell, round and firm, upon other people's ears. Our words—fervent, misbehaved, fatal wounds, survivors of everything—rose up for all to see. It's not that things had been calm before, but to the voices that had already risen, those of the women in the fields of art and culture were added, taking a stance together. Everything in those days became ours, because it was easy to say, I am here, I know what this is about. Our stories, mixed together. Our voices, simultaneous. It was difficult to distinguish between what was your own and what was everyone else's, we will say with a wide smile on our lips, inspired by community.

We had lived for decades under the frightening grind of femicide. Our mothers were dying, our sisters, our cousins, our neighbors were all dying, even our enemies were dying. Everyone was dying; they didn't stop dying. We got used to looking at one another with the grieving eyes of survivors. We wrote essays, we joined activist groups, we included more women on our class syllabi, we raised our voices in countless marches. But there they were, they followed us everywhere, those ever-increasing statistics: Three women a day. Six women a day. Nine women a day. By January 2019 ten women a day were murdered in Mexico. It was impossible not to wonder when it would happen to me. When it would happen to you, who looks at me, who is at my side. When will they kill us?

When the law of silence reigned, those killings seemed like somewhat anomalous eruptions in an inexplicably or irremediably violent world. But the stories uncovered by the Mexican #MeToo movement brought to light and made evident the link between everyday violence and crime of spectacle. Every act of violence counts. There is only one small step—not a quantum leap—between domestic abuse, workplace inequality, daily harassment, sexual assault, economic mortification, cultural belittlement, a lack of opportunities, and the murder of hundreds of thousands of women in Mexico and throughout the entire world.

Did we know these stories? Of course we did, sometimes through word of mouth, sometimes in our own flesh. It started with stories from #MiPrimerAcoso and #RopaSucia, activism initiatives that circulated women's stories online. Was everyone else already aware? Of course they were, sometimes through word of mouth, sometimes in their own flesh. And beyond the screens, there were the many support groups, the mothers of the disappeared, the #MareaVerde movement, those who said Ni Una Más (Not one more), to remind us of it. Thus, amplifying voices and echoing the cries of countless others, all these stories materializing in sounds and letters, with both real and false names in the public sphere, including Twitter, took on a weight that in many ways felt like horror. We will say in the future that we bowed our heads, even wished that it wasn't real. It was a world founded on women's silence. It was a world that required the most intimate silence from women—their demise—to keep functioning.

And then, we will say, it took off.

One woman began to speak, and another followed her, and another followed her, and another. They were quite young, we will recall, but their stories were not unlike those that came before them, as if everything had only gotten worse over time. We knew it immediately: no one was going to stop the movement and no one was going to contain it. To exceed. To overflow. To get out of control. That is a social movement. Nobody participates in a revolt by raising their hand and waiting for their turn to speak. What comes to light is human and terrifying, we will say, recalling that poem by Ilya Kaminsky that we had heard read in a salon or a warehouse full of people yearning for its immediate translation, its proliferation—yes, we lived happily during the war too.

For years we didn't want the war, but wherever we turned, there it was, with its mass graves. With our disappeared. And with their money, yes. With that too. But we no longer wanted to live happily during the war. We took to the streets together and marched, too, with everyone by our sides, in different groupings and packs, against that false happiness of the war. Some men recognized our plight and asked for forgiveness; others got scared. Others remained silent. And then, among the pain and anxiety, among the fervor and agitation, April dawned and the movement experienced severe backlash when Armando Vega Gil, the musician from Botellita de Jerez, the band from the eighties and nineties that many of us learned about with irreverence and confidence, took his own life after reading an accusation of assault on @MeTooMusicaMX. In the future, we will have to say this with deep consternation, with a shared pain. In the future, we will pause and remember his words: "It is correct that women raise their voice so that our rotten world will change."

And so, at the beginning of April, the cruelest month, the voice, the presence, the demand for justice became even more important. We will say that. We had all lost so much because of the silence and silencing of women. And if some were beaten back into silence, while others clung even more to the authoritarian and violent ways of the war, there were also those who demanded we continue, with hard facts, with radical empathy, with an ethics of care as our banner. There were tears within the movement and at assemblies, we will recall. There was dissent. There was perplexity. There were long hours of contemplation. And a lot of work, hours of dialogue and research, entire days spent exchanging information and discussing strategies. There were open hands. And this frenzied, lively, collective energy is what made it possible to keep living to achieve this future—in which the laws that guarantee a world without violence against women are enforced, the protocols for workplaces free of assault are respected, girls and boys have equal access to education, women and men receive equal pay, a world in which six or nine or ten of us no longer die each day—but it still depends on what we do today. It is not a more comfortable world, but one in which everything will be reevaluated, under the protection of all eyes, all bodies, because it affects all of us. That world, this possible future, requires all of our intelligence, knowledge, tenderness, disagreement, and wonder. That world requires all this of you and me. Now. Here. Because not one more death—ni una más—and not one less life—ni una menos—is to be spared.

XXVI

Touching Is a Verb: The Hands of the Pandemic and Its Inescapable Questions

Emergency Brake

From Walter Benjamin: "Marx says that revolutions are the locomotive of world history. But perhaps it is quite otherwise. Perhaps revolutions are an attempt by the passengers on this train—namely, the human race—to activate the emergency brake."[1] I mention it here because everything in these days of pandemic seems to be carried out in that unprecedented time inaugurated by the pulling of an emergency brake: the deceleration. It does not, of course, have anything to do with the romantic slowness some novelists and activists have written about, but a vulnerable impasse in which hypervigilance and anxiety predominate. The pandemic is not a haven. Much less a safe one. We have stopped short, certainly, and though it is clear that the hand that pulled the brake is a human hand—climate change and the alteration of earth's ecosystems are the very form of the savage capitalocene—it is less clear whether that brake will be enough to transform an economic system that, in its effort to produce the greatest profit possible, has systematically devastated the earth. The false premise of *normalcy*—the conditions that supposedly predated the pandemic—is at the root of the problem that led to the coronavirus pandemic known as COVID-19. And the impossibility of returning to it, to that veneer of normalcy, even if some wanted to, is frequently reiterated. As Angela Davis and Rita Segato have argued, the possibility is now emerging of replacing that old normalcy with a world of transversed solidarities in which we become aware how our material and affective interdependence rests on the earth itself.

A Mere Approximation

We are not going through a revolution but through a change that is so radical, so circulated throughout every corner of the planet, that we might even call it a structural change. We don't know how long the transformation will last or what consequences it will bring or how long those consequences will be felt, but we experience these days of pandemic with the anxiety and curiosity of those who witness a phenomenon without the precise language to describe it, for which a vocabulary to comprehend it does not yet exist. We live with the hypervigilance button turned on. We are foreigners who, tossed without luggage into an unknown city, strain to create analogies to be able to visualize—and understanding is much more complicated—what is happening before our eyes. *This is like . . . It could well be about . . .*

The translation process, which includes the experience and the language in which this experience is enunciated, is arduous, frankly often impenetrable. In every attempt you can see that language does not match the unprecedented contexts and phenomena that, whether obviously or subtly, obey rules that are not yet clear to us. Every attempt is just an approximation.

Touching Is a Verb

As the virus is spread through proximity, especially through breath and touch, we have been compelled to become more aware of our bodies. It seems like a simple operation. It isn't. The contemporary means of capitalist production, that cold, calculated machine, has accustomed us to living under the illusion that we are incorporeal. We can work endlessly. We can consume endlessly. If we were in a story by the Salvadoran writer Claudia Hernández, we would be those characters who, even when dead, even when already turned into walking cadavers, continue swiping our entry card to get into work or pulling out our credit card at cash registers. US capitalism is like this: literally disembodied.

The illusion of not having a body, supported in part by the widespread consumption of pills and various medications, leads to the perception that we have no other connection to the world besides the technological. From the spell of abstraction hangs the absence of solidarity with our surroundings, and at the end of it all, indolence. That which does not touch us—that which we do not know touches us—does not hurt us. But now that we are stopped, now that we know that our hands are lethal weapons and not just, as Kant wanted, what differentiates us from animals, we cannot not think about it. The rematerialization of our worlds in times of deceleration forces questions that are political at their very root: Who else has touched this object that I am touching? Which is another way of asking: Where does it come from, who produces it, in what conditions of exploitation or sanitation is this thing in my hands created, with what quantity of virus? It took the anthropologist Anna Lowenhaupt Tsing years and many pages to answer those questions in relation to the matsutake, a revered Japanese mushroom that grows in wooded zones that have survived processes of devastation.[2] Indeed, there are a ton of hands described in her book *The Mushroom at the End of the World*: those of migrant workers, those of businessmen, those of forest rangers, those of police, those of immigration agents. Calloused hands and soft hands. Hands accustomed to caresses, hands that have never felt the relief of moisturizing lotion. To trace the labor of hands in the processes of production and reproduction in our world—this is an intimately political task. And right now it's an inescapable task. In fact, our lives depend on asking these questions and paying full attention to the answers. Everything we have close by—and right now we know that we are always, that we always have been, close to so many other hands—affects us because it implicates us. This could well open the door to the end of indolence.

The Rematerialization of Domestic Space

Stripped of supposedly secure or fixed daily routines, expelled from the hustle that made factories and banks and universities run on time, condemned to homebound sedentariness without the security of a salary, or forced to work in unsanitary conditions just to keep the engine whirring (if at minimum speed), we have been brought face to face with deceleration by COVID-19. Here we go, from the beginning of the day, checking statistics that are increasingly alarming, heeding new security measures. Meanwhile, many of us inhabit homes that before were only places to stop for a few hours, almost always at night, sleeping somewhat restlessly. Suddenly, that space that we referred to as *house*, as *my house* or *our house*, unfolds into unexplored corners and things out of place. It's a strange entity, released from itself, that we must slowly get accustomed, or reaccustomed, to. Sweeping, mopping, washing dishes, making the bed, putting clothes in the washing machine, dusting—all those daily activities that, at least in this house, in our house, we've always taken care of ourselves—frequently fall on the shoulders of women and usually go unnoticed. The impossibility of leaving the house, and thus the impossibility of ignoring these homemaking routines, makes them monumental. In fact, it transforms them into the skeleton of the day, the only structure that endures when everything else has fallen down the rabbit hole.

The time previously consumed by moving from one place to another, even to eat, we now occupy by carefully selecting the goods with which to cook on a daily basis. We must carefully wash each vegetable and fruit. We must soak beans the night ahead. We must calculate how many days the rice will last us. Between each task, we must wash our hands again and again, for twenty seconds that, when carefully observed, constitute one of the better parts of the day. In Houston, quarantine obliges us to stay at home, but it does not yet prohibit us from going to the grocery store to gather provisions or walk the dog (as long as you maintain a safe distance from other walkers). The restaurants, which have closed, still prepare food to go. But in these times, when we have to think about all the hands involved in food preparation, it's best to pass on that opportunity. We would like to do it, above all to support local restaurants, which are having a difficult time, but we still cannot persuade ourselves. Cooking, furthermore, is not an activity that lends itself to speed. Things do not hurry up or slow down according to the whims of the chef. Everything takes its time. The vegetables, the grains, the fruits. And part of the rematerialization of our homes consists in finding the rhythm of things, their own ways of being in time.

Those of us who are not detained in prisons or asylums, or stuck outside on the streets, are now inside, faced with furniture, spoons, mirrors that daily life had rendered invisible or mundane, but which now recover their presence. Treating someone like a piece of furniture, recalls the theorist Sara Ahmed in *Queer Phenomenology*, means treating them as if they do not truly exist.[3] It means they are ignored. In a disembodied environment, the natural place of furniture is that of discretion if not the most cunning invisibility. Quite the contrary, *queer* objects—that uncomfortable chair, that conspicuous table—do not fade into the background. *Queer* objects resist disappearing into the scenery. The pandemic, which hasn't let us forget the material limit of our experience, has also forced our gaze, all of our senses, to recognize the objects we depend on for their use value (and not their exchange value). The pans, chipped, almost devoid of Teflon. The fly swatter. The living room sofa, which had never really been used, has been relocated to the kitchen bar, where it's possible to lie down and read something while the water boils. The soles of shoes, with traces of the outdoors, that we leave at the entryway. The materiality of the home surrounds us, encloses us, some are even suffocated by it, but at the end of the day it's here, physical and solid, against the squalls of information and fear, in an unshakable you against the abstraction of the state and capital, inciting them or compelling them to know they are a body of our body.

The Solitude Is Real

In the United States it's common to invite people to parties during set hours: from 5:00 to 7:00 p.m., for example; from 6:00 to 9:00 p.m.; or even later, when there's a real desire to let loose. Street protests require a permit that not only includes a schedule but also specific routes. Students and employees eat salads from plastic containers in front of computers or telephones while they check their messages or watch videos. No one arrives at the office doors that line narrow hallways, always lit, without calling first. Or homes. Truman Capote said that he went to New York to be alone, but I wouldn't be so provincial. Now that remote existence has become the daily method of work, it's impossible not to see these interactions we experience via strictly regulated absences. We are accompanied by a profound solitude. The rhythms of the empire's production are only possible through isolated bodies whose desires or needs are satisfied immediately and automatically so as to not stop the flow of things. The pandemic has also rematerialized this primoradial absence, making clear that we are enclosed by empty space in every direction. Teachers have noticed that they're more exhausted after one hour of class on Zoom than five hours of in-person teaching. The reason is simple but sepulchral: it seems like we're there, all together, talking and creating, seeing each other, but the body knows we aren't actually. This distance, the body's acknowledgment of it, exhausts. That dissonance leaves us with our mouths hanging open. This distance, which far precedes the pandemic, becomes intolerable in it. We now resent the separation precipitated by these days only because we cannot stop seeing it. We cannot play dumb to the body in so many different ways. Perhaps that's why we've returned to the phone call: we complained that the sound of the voice disconnected from facial gestures or bodily movements was incapable of generating a sense of closeness. But it's now clear to us that the mechanism of the voice, when accompanied by the stipulated choreography of Skype or Zoom, is even poorer. Now that I talk to my parents on the phone every day—they're old and in another city—their voices alone, their even and full voices, with their inflections and hesitations, with those tones that I recognize well, produce an intense intimacy, capable of unleashing the imagination of the other senses.

Everything Is Different through a Window

The border of a home is its door, but the most interesting phenomena happen through the windows. That's where what is perceived, but still not reached, exists. Desire is its other name. A window is a passage, often a secret passage. *Discern* is a verb that occurs through glass. Although many imagine Houston as a dry place because of its association with the aridity of Texas, this place is, as Gabriela Wiener once rightly described it, the Amazon itself. The humidity and sultry air make it favorable for the proliferation of oaks and magnolia trees, vines and ferns, bougainvillea and bamboo. They were here before, of course, but they're more noticeable now that the gardeners have stopped coming and the plants grow as they will. The variety of their greens explodes on median strips and gardens, empty lots and back patios. The shadows that the trees produce are cast, precisely, over the imperfections of the pavement. An enormous beetle just passed by, noisily, with its wings extended. The butterflies, which chase each other around, crash into fences in an act of mere distraction. The reduction of fast-paced city noises, of the cars above all, has allowed other sounds to approximate our ears as if they were new. The birds, seen from afar, are varied and magnificent, and also rematerialize as they pass by with their unprecedented uproar. The cat meows. The dog barks. The cooing of pigeons. The buzzing of insects. These two, three, four, five, six chickens that smugly walk down the street as if it were a giant corral. Is that the crowing of a rooster in the middle of the afternoon? What I mean is that never like in these days has that interconnection been so clear between animals and plants and the twists and turns of the city, which is only half-urban. Or whose urbanity is a complicated network of negotiations with nature that, at the slightest neglect, shows its face or returns. If the window is border, border-like events are also what take place in front of it.

Recovering Our Feet

In *WALL-E*, the 2008 animated science-fiction film, there is a scene that portrays the hyperconsumerist world of the United States. If you recall from the postapocalyptic context of the film, a large part of humanity lives in the Axiom, where people's desires and needs are automatically and immediately satisfied. Those humans watch so much television and sit for so much time that they've lost the use of their legs. Thus, a specific behavior (being a couch potato) has reconfigured the human body, mutilating it in some way. Frankensteins of the capitalocene. In cities like Houston, dominated by a landscape of numerous six-lane highways, sometimes even wider, it's easier to live without walking. In fact, the most difficult thing in a city designed for the circulation of automated vehicles is to walk. After five o'clock, after many people's work day, the center of Houston is and has been a desolate territory to pass through, frequented only by homeless people and those who are lost. It's the landscape after the daily battle: a shell of vacant buildings where the amber spark of electricity never stops glowing.

We live in a traditionally Mexican neighborhood on one side of the I-45 and, even though it's only a thirty-minute walk to the university, it's rare to see students or professors crossing the urban space. The sanitary measures of the pandemic, which allow people to go out but without close contact, have brought out the solitary tribes from their homes and placed them on semi-empty streets where other solitary tribes sit on their porches or in their front yards, which they seem to be enjoying for the first time. The mild climate of this spring helps, of course, but there is something about that slow walking of socially distanced groups that makes everything different. Never before have people so often raised their hands from afar in greeting or goodbye, either way in recognition of another. Never before have parents and children walked along the same sidewalk. Together. There are people with masks, but on bicycles. Attached to leashes, dogs walk the Houston streets over and over again.

Perhaps it isn't strange that the echo of Spanish reverberates so clearly on these pandemic walks. What's there, before us and under our feet, isn't a road of standardized and swift production. It isn't a road of the enclosed cars, protecting the labor of their air conditioners. It is a domestic street, if you can call it that. As the public sphere retreats, the rules of interior physicality—which state, among other things, that we must not forget that we are bodies—go out the window, injecting a pedestrian velocity into everything that happens. As if the rematerialization of the home had poured first into the garden, then onto the sidewalk, then into the streets as spillover. The streets are solitary, it's true, but they look, paradoxically, fuller than ever. That's where all of us who have recovered our feet go.

Potency

It's true that the number of infections and deaths is increasing, as is the rate of unemployment. Enclosed in our domestic spaces, our bodies have stopped presenting themselves to the communion of the market except to acquire the most basic things: food, cleaning products, water. We already knew it, but we confirm it to ourselves: those who produce the basic goods, those who keep us alive, are immigrants, who, even considering the recent essential workers stamp, still don't have documents, or even worse, health insurance. In addition to doctors and nurses, we depend on those who harvest lettuce and eggplants, the grocery-store cashier, those who clean the bodies of the elderly, those who fix washing machines, those who deliver mail. The rest of us couldn't be here, digitally fulfilling our roles, if there weren't men and women out there, bent over vast vegetable fields, risking their lives to, paradoxically, keep living.

I work at a public university whose majority Latinx student population has made it, officially, a Hispanic-serving institution. This means that many of our students are the first of their working families to attend college. Perhaps some of them are children or grandchildren of men and women who have dedicated their lives to picking beets or lettuce. This also means that many of them have one or two jobs in order to survive, pay rent and tuition, all the while contributing to their households. The pandemic has hit them with a special furor. But it isn't strange to me that, although they face major challenges—some have lost their jobs and some have been threatened with eviction orders—they are still fighting, attending classes through digital platforms hurriedly and efficiently organized by the university. We aren't reinventing the wheel, but adapting a more flexible system, especially regarding the class schedule, to facilitate their participation. I don't know if they will become writers, but they write in Spanish in this class; they write creatively, expressing critical views about our world and the status quo, both in the United States and Latin America, as well as about other, possible futures. Sofía writes about a young gymnast who never gives up. Rony about a general who represses activists in Central America. Jessica about twins who have to get used to living in peace. Alan about an athlete who, once he has accepted that his team has lost a soccer game, begins to mentally prepare himself for the next season. Linda about a young woman who finally accepts herself. Jonathan about a woman who prepares for her return to Chile. There aren't moral lessons in their stories or reiterations of an identity that has burst in a thousand different ways, but the traces of a vast and critical experience that will illuminate our futurity. Reading their writing keeps me alert. Seeing them react to the texts keeps me alert. Because it isn't only the writing itself that wakes me up, hopeful, but also the way they talk to one another: the care of their readings and the care of their opinions. This awareness of the state of vulnerability that we share when we pull out a text and offer it to others. If these young people in serious predicaments are capable of such responsibility and such care, if they are capable of giving so much of themselves during such difficult times, I believe they are capable of anything. And then I can sleep at night.

Toward a Visceral State

When my university made the announcement that it was extending spring break to prepare for the transition to remote education and to take other measures against the dissemination of the coronavirus, I knew this thing was serious and would arrive soon. At that moment I was walking with my mother, a healthy woman of seventy-six, through the streets of our neighborhood in Houston. I had walked a little ahead of her to read the university's announcement on my phone, and when I finished, I turned back to look at her. She walked with those long strides her legs still allow her. Her head was bent forward, paying attention to the imperfections in her path so as to avoid any kind of fall. I had gotten used to those daily walks during which, under the pretext of health, we talked about everything. I told her immediately, knowing how much I would undoubtedly miss her: You have to go back to Mexico (speaking to her using the *usted*, like all good border women). My decision was immediate and the reason simple: here on a tourist visa, my mother lacked the health insurance that would allow her to be admitted to a hospital if she got sick. Without that document, she would be rejected, as so many others are, at the doors of any health establishment. This is what it is to live in a country that lacks any public health system and that insists on protecting the large pharmaceuticals rather than the well-being of the human population. Since she was employed by the Universidad Autónoma del Estado de México for a large part of her life, she enjoys a meager pension, one that includes medical services that, until now, have been fundamental to her life as an elderly adult. (The three surgeries she had to save her from a ruptured aneurysm were done, for example, in a neurology hospital in Mexico City with an unbeatable quality of care and for which she didn't have to pay a dollar out of pocket.) But here, on this side of the border, my mother shares the eviscerated destiny of the thousands and thousands of people who must frequently resort to home remedies in order to take care of themselves—when possible, with the support of medications that some relative or friend brings from Mexico. The number of times I've witnessed the informal exchange of B12 vitamins, antibiotics, or antihistamines—medications that do not cure illnesses but offer relief to people who do not have the luxury to stop working, even for a day—is astounding.

My mother agreed with me and we acted immediately. We made the necessary arrangements that day for her to meet her sisters at the border before returning home. Two days later, my mother boarded a plane that deposited her in the capital of a country where, in spite of everything happening there, she is safer. The statistics have shown that COVID-19 not only attacks elderly people with particular viciousness but also other precarious and marginalized populations—precisely those who cannot cover health insurance expenses and for whom an infection can be a death sentence.

Like a giant X-ray, the deceleration the pandemic has brought makes clear, or even exaggerates, what was already present: an economic system guided by profit at the expense of everything else and a Visceraless State—that is, a state for which bodies are not a matter of care but merely extraction. The worst that could happen to us, Arundhati Roy convincingly argues, is to return to that savage normality.[4] And I add: to that merciless world which, imprisoned by the evil spell of disembodiment, is incapable of recognizing the ties of reciprocity that unite us with others and with the earth. Indeed, the inescapable awareness of a material closeness with others might come mixed with anxiety and unease, but also with potentiality. Another world is possible, that's what life clearly tells us when it imposes itself over the pandemic. Will it be possible then, from all this experience with illness, to overthrow that visceraless normalcy once and for all and participate, at the same time, in the emergence of a state with heart and flesh, muscle and cartilage? In other words, how will we resolve to demand that the state comply with its responsibility to protect the health of the population while we simultaneously produce embodied relations, that is, modes of affect and connection that stem from the broad admission that we are bodies, that we need and can provide care? It is evident to me that, at least in the United States, this struggle begins and is intimately tied to the absence of a public health system that, by not existing, has sentenced a large number of workers to routine death, and especially essential workers—and now the pandemic has also confirmed this status—many of whom continue to be considered illegal by this incompetent and genocidal government. In that sense, the fight for a public health system and the fight for migration reform are, in reality, the same fight; both are centered primarily on the fundamental assertion that we are bodies, and consequently, on the basic fact that so many bodies depend on each other in seriously altered ecological contexts. The macro measures—changes to public health on a state level—should not go against and, in fact, must complement smaller, quotidian community measures; and these together might be able to unlock the harmful alliance of state and corporation, and their intrusion on our health system. On its own, the pandemic, which has helped us clearly see the brutal disposition of our time, will not create visceral relations—embodied relations, with others, in material connection to our communities—that could well lay the groundwork for another reality. We would do well to attend to the questions that rematerialization compels, and in fact makes inescapable. The beginning of the end of indolence depends on these answers. And that is something.

XXVII

Keep Writing

Because we become social in language. My *I* for *you*. Your *you* for *me*. Our *y'all* for *them*.

Because writing, by nature, invites us to consider the possibility that the world can, in fact, be different.

Because the secret mechanism of writing is imagination.

Because a manta is hung here that clearly reads "Writing exists out there, right in front of you, as you walk about the world and in your imagination."

Because *imagination* is another word for *criticism* and, this, the other word for *subversion*.

Because those who write will never adapt.

Because perhaps the heart of writing consists in no more than showing your face and, if necessary, offering the other cheek. Poetry does not impose, Paul Celan says, it exposes. But these are minor things. Because to confront is, above all, to confront death. To place yourself in pursuit of the unknown or the darkness, which is the same thing. In that ethical and aesthetic attitude of the exposition that opens, and upon opening, damages; there, where the certainty urgently emerges that death, independent of its circumstance, is an act of violence; there, on that path, both the face and poetry walk alone. They are alone. Because of that, too.

Because memory.

Because writing teaches us that nothing is "natural." Things are closer than they appear, writing also tells us this.

Because it is through that rectangular artifact we call a book that we communicate with our dead. And all of the dead are our dead.

Because a sentence produces memories that will be inhabited forever by the names of Marco and José Luis Piña Dávila, Ciudad Juárez, Chihuahua, January 30, 2010.

Because the contour of a page shows us the limits of reality.

Because a manta is hung here that reads "Tell them not to kill me."

Because belonging is something I do through you, sentence.

Because at the end of each line there is an abyss worth tumbling into. Or launching yourself into. Or disappearing into.

Because look how the verb *to burst* bursts out of itself.

Because, too, it is what we would write in the case that we were to write.

Because, in its role as a word, each word questions the customs of our perception.

Because a line is an imprecation or a prayer.

Because terror stops there, where the word *terror* stops, inscribed.

Because there are voices that come from afar, from below, from beyond.

Because using language, or letting yourself be used by it, is a daily political practice. Disrupting the limits of the intelligible or the real, writing's very purpose, is to be political. Independent of the subject addressed or the anecdote told or the stylistic challenge proposed, the written text is a concrete exercise in politics. My hand, primarily the left though also the right, is purely political. That.

Because within books I always greet the unfamiliar that I've become so familiar with.

Because a sentence produces memories that will be inhabited forever by the name of Lucila Quintanilla, Monterrey, Nuevo León, October 6, 2010.

Because everything starts, indeed, with a sign.

Because a paragraph is an extreme sport.

Because words are necessary to say, I do not extend my hand to you, Señor Presidente. I cannot welcome you.

Because language is a form of opposition that always takes us elsewhere; to that other, unthinkable place inside ourselves.

Because it is only through writing that the here is founded. Because the now.

Because while the violence invades and acquires unprecedented forms, contemporary language has difficulty giving it plausible names: Martín and Bryan Almanza; Nuevo Laredo–Reynosa–Matamoros, April 2010.

Because in the rectangle of a page I am nourished and I dream and I plunge and I die. Because there, too, I am reborn. We are reborn.

Because the word *shard*, the word *soldier*, the word *impunity*.

Because this is the most definitive form of the collective.

Because a manta is hung here with the story of the woman who makes paper flowers to bring to the cemetery at the end of every month, waiting for justice, demanding justice.

Because when faced with the questions: Is it worth it to get up early in the morning just to keep writing? Can writing, in fact, be something that acts against fear or terror? Since when has a page stopped a bullet? Has someone ever used a book as a shield over their chest, just above their heart? Is there a protected zone, somehow invincible, around a written text? Is it possible, not to mention desirable, to grip or wield or raise a word? My answer continues to be yes.

Because *yes* is a small and sacred and savage word all at the same time.

Because, frankly, I don't know how to do anything else.

Because a manta is hung here that reads "We are a country in mourning."

Because within these words continue to beat the names of the forty-one children who died at the ABC Day Care in Hermosillo, Sonora, 2009.

Because what. And because yes. And, well, these.

Because a sentence produces memories that will be inhabited forever by the name Liliana Rivera Garza, Azcapotzalco, Mexico City, July 16, 1990.

Because I do not forget. Because I will not forget. Because we will never forget.

Endnotes

Introduction

1. Adriana Cavarero, *Horrorism: Naming Contemporary Violence*, trans. William McCuaig (New York: Columbia University Press, 2009).
2. Adela Cedillo, "Intersections between the Dirty War and the War on Drugs in Northwestern Mexico (1969–1985)," PhD diss. (Madison: University of Wisconsin–Madison, 2019).
3. Translator's note: The Spanish *estado sin entrañas* plays with the linguistic link between the terms *entraña* (or, entrails, insides, organs) and *entrañable* (or, endearing), thus creating a connection between flesh and care. The neologism *visceraless* is meant to similarly express both internal organs and a sense of a close, structural relationship. A visceral reaction to something is used to express not an intellectual feeling but a deeper, corporeal one. A Visceraless State is one that lacks a political acknowledgment of the human body and its individual subjectivity.
4. Giorgio Agamben, *The Open: Man and Animal*, trans. Kevin Attell (Stanford, CA: Stanford University Press, 2004).
5. Tony Judt, *Ill Fares the Land* (New York: Penguin Press, 2010).
6. Oswaldo Zavala, *Los cárteles no existen: Narcotráfico y cultura en México* (Barcelona: Malpaso, 2018).
7. Cavarero, *Horrorism*, 34.
8. Edmond Jabès, *From the Desert to the Book: Dialogues with Marcel Cohen*, trans. Pierre Joris (New York: Station Hill Press, 1990).

9. See, for example, Daniela Rea's *Nadie les pidió perdón* (2016), Marcela Turati's *Fuego cruzado: Las víctimas atrapadas en la guerra del narco* (2011), Federico Mastrogiovanni's *El asesino que no seremos* (2018), and John Gibler's *I Couldn't Even Imagine That They Would Kill Us: An Oral History of the Attacks against the Students of Ayotzinapa* (2017), and the collectively written *Ayotzinapa: La travesía de las tortugas* (2015).

10. Jacques Rancière, "The Intolerable Image," in *The Emancipated Spectator*, trans. Gregory Elliot (London: Verso, 2011), 97.

11. Jacques Rancière, "The Paradoxes of Political Art," in *Dissensus: On Politics and Aesthetics*, trans. and ed. Steven Corcoran (London, New York: Continuum, 2010), 139.

12. Rancière, "The Misadventures of Critical Thought," in *The Emancipated Spectator*, 49.

13. Rancière, "The Intolerable Image," 103.

The Claimant

1. Luz María Dávila confronted President Felipe Calderón when he visited Ciudad Juárez on February 11, 2010. Journalist Sandra Rodríguez Nieto quoted her words in an article in *El diario de Juárez*, from which, in turn, I quoted them. Text in bold belongs to Luz María Dávila; text in italics to Sandra Rodríguez. The rest combines words, especially adjectives, from Ramón López Velarde's poetry and my own writing.

The Visceraless State

1. Viviane Forrester, *The Economic Horror*, trans. Sheila Malovany-Chevallier (Malden, MA: Blackwell Publishers Inc., 1999).

War and Imagination

1. Kiran Desai, *The Inheritance of Loss* (New York: Atlantic Monthly Press, 2006), 157.

2. Desai, *The Inheritance of Loss*, 158.

3. Andrés Molina Enríquez, *Los grandes problemas nacionales* (Mexico: Carranza e Hijos, 1909).
4. Francisco I. Madero, *The Presidential Succession of 1910*, trans. Thomas B. Davis (New York: P. Lang, 1990).
5. Mariano Azuela, *The Underdogs: A Novel of the Mexican Revolution*, trans. Sergio Waisman (New York: Penguin Classics, 2008).
6. Nellie Campobello, *Cartucho. Relatos de la lucha en el norte de México* (Mexico: Ediciones integrales, 1931).
7. Sara Ahmed, *The Cultural Politics of Emotion* (New York: Routledge, 2004), 62–81.
8. Susan Sontag, et. al, "Tuesday, and After," *New Yorker* (September 24, 2001).
9. Alessandro Baricco, *An Iliad*, trans. Ann Goldstein (New York: Knopf, 2006).

On *Diary of Pain* by María Luisa Puga

1. María Luisa Puga, *Diario del dolor* (Mexico: Alfaguara, 2004).
2. Puga, *Diario*, 37.
3. Puga, *Diario*, 90.
4. Puga, *Diario*, 22.
5. Puga, *Diario*, 35.
6. Puga, *Diario*, 53–54.
7. Judith Butler, *Precarious Life: The Powers of Mourning and Violence* (New York: Verso, 2004).

Tragic Agency

1. Susan Sontag, *Regarding the Pain of Others* (New York: Farrar, Straus and Giroux, 2003).
2. John Drakakis and Naomi Conn Liebler, eds., "Introduction," in *Tragedy* (New York: Longman, 1998), 2.
3. Drakakis and Liebler, "Introduction," 3.
4. Karl Jaspers, *Tragedy Is Not Enough*, trans. Harald A. T. Reiche, Harry T. Moore, and Karl W. Deutsch (Boston: Beacon Press, 1952), 57.

5. Raymond Williams, *Modern Tragedy* (Stanford, CA: Stanford University Press, 1966), 202–3.
6. Williams, *Modern Tragedy*, 64.
7. Arthur Kleinman, Veena Das, and Margaret Lock, eds., *Social Suffering* (Berkeley: University of California Press, 1997), ix.
8. Jorge Luis Borges, *This Craft of Verse*, ed. Călin-Andrei Mihăilescu (Cambridge, MA: Harvard University Press, 2000), 45.

I Won't Let Anyone Say Those Are the Best Years of Your Life

1. Paul Nizan, *Aden, Arabie*, trans. Joan Pinkham (New York: Monthly Review Press, 1968), 59.
2. *Estos últimos años en Ciudad Juárez* (Santa Fe, NM: Brown Buffalo Press, 2020). Unless otherwise noted, all quoted material in this chapter cite this work, originally written in Spanish, and translated into English by the author.

On *2501 Migrants* by Alejandro Santiago

1. Karl Marx, *Economic and Philosophic Manuscripts of 1884*, trans. Martin Milligan (Moscow: Foreign Languages Pub. House, 1959).
2. Juan Rulfo, *Pedro Páramo*, trans. Margaret Sayers Peden (New York: Grove Press, 1994), 3.
3. Marx, *Economic*, 108.
4. Emmanuel Levinas, "The Philosopher and Death," in *Alterity and Transcendence*, trans. Michael B. Smith (New York: Columbia University Press, 1999), 163.
5. Mike Davis, *City of Quartz: Excavating the Future in Los Angeles* (New York: Verso, 1990).
6. Laura Velasco Ortiz, "Agentes étnicos transnacionales: Las organizaciones de indígenas migrantes en la frontera México–Estados Unidos," *Estudios Sociológicos* 20, no. 2 (May–August 2002): 335–69.

What Country Is This, Agripina?

1. Juan Rulfo, "Luvina," *The Plain in Flames*, trans. Ilan Stavans (Austin: University of Texas Press, 2012), 70.
2. Rulfo, "Luvina," 70.
3. Rulfo, "Luvina," 73.
4. Rulfo, "Luvina," 73.

Desiccated Mermaids

1. Bernardino de Sahagún, *General History of the Things of New Spain: Florentine Codex*, trans. Arthur J. O. Anderson and Charles E. Dibble (Santa Fe, NM, and Salt Lake City: School of American Research and University of Utah Press, 1982), 89.
2. José Antonio Trejo Sánchez and Emilio Gerardo Arriaga, "Memoria colectiva: Vida lacustre y reserva simbólica en el Valle de Toluca, Estado de México," *Convergencia* 16, no. 50 (2009): 308.
3. Trejo Sánchez and Gerardo Arriaga, "Memoria," 313.

The War We Lost

1. Adriana Cavarero, *Horrorism: Naming Contemporary Violence*, trans. William McCuaig (New York: Columbia University Press, 2009).
2. Julio Scherer García, "Proceso en la guarida de 'El Mayo' Zambada," *Proceso*, April 3, 2010, https://www.proceso.com.mx/106967/proceso-en-la-guarida-de-el-mayo-zambada.
3. Gabriela Warkentin, "El periodista, el capo y la foto," *El País*, April 8, 2010, https://elpais.com/internacional/2010/04/08/actualidad/1270677607_850215.html.

The Neo-Camelias

1. Arturo Pérez-Reverte, *The Queen of the South*, trans. Andrew Hurley (New York: G. P. Putnam's Sons, 2004).

A Network of Holes

1. Peter Sloterdijk, *Bubbles: Spheres Volume I*, trans. Wieland Hoban (Los Angeles: Semiotext[e]), 164.

Mourning

1. Cristina Rivera Garza, "La vida precariat," *Letras libres*, October 31, 2004, https://www.letraslibres.com/mexico/libros/la-vida-precaria.
2. Javier Sicilia, "Carta abierta a políticos y criminals," *Proceso*, April 3, 2011, https://www.proceso.com.mx/266990/javier-sicilia-carta-abierta-a-politicos-y-criminales.
3. Judith Butler, "Violence, Mourning, Politics," *Precarious Life: The Powers of Mourning and Violence* (New York: Verso, 2004).
4. Butler, *Precarious Life*, 28.
5. Butler, *Precarious Life*, 21–22.
6. Butler, *Precarious Life*, 28.
7. Butler, *Precarious Life*, 22.
8. Butler, *Precarious Life*, 49.

Writing in Migration

1. Annie Ernaux, *The Years*, trans. Allison L. Strayer (New York: Seven Stories Press, 2017).
2. Lina Meruane, *Volverse Palestina* (Barcelona: Literatura Random House, 2015).
3. José Revueltas, *Human Mourning*, trans. Roberto Crespi (Minneapolis: University of Minnesota Press, 1990), 62–63.
4. Gloria Anzaldúa, *Borderlands/La Frontera: The New Mestiza* (San Francisco: Aunt Lute Books, 2012), 33.

Writing against War

1. Joe Sacco, *Safe Area Goražde* (Seattle: Fantagraphics Books, 2000), 79.
2. Christopher Hitchens, "Introduction," *Safe Area Goražde*.

Touching Is a Verb

1. Walter Benjamin, "Paralipomena to 'On the Concept of History,'" *Walter Benjamin: Selected Writings*, volume 4, trans. Edmund Jephcott and Others, ed. Howard Eiland and Michael W. Jennings (Cambridge, MA: Belknap Press of Harvard University Press, 1996), 401–11.

2. Anna Lowenhaupt Tsing, *The Mushroom at the End of the World: On the Possibility of Life in Capitalist Ruins* (Princeton, NJ: Princeton University Press, 2015).

3. Sara Ahmed, *Queer Phenomenology: Orientations, Objects, Others* (Durham, NC: Duke University Press, 2006).

4. Arundhati Roy, "The Pandemic Is a Portal," *Financial Times*, April 3, 2020, https://www.ft.com/content/10d8f5e8-74eb-11ea-95fe-fcd274e920ca.

Credits

I Won't Let Anyone Say Those Are the Best Years of Your Life (p. 42). Written in English by the author and appearing here for the first time.

On *2501 Migrants* by Alejandro Santiago (p. 53). A version of this English translation was first published in July 2018 in *Asymptote*.

Nonfiction (p. 63). A version of this English translation was first published in 2019 in *Washington Square Review*.

The Morning After (p. 82). First published in Spanish on November 9, 2016, in *Literal Magazine*.

On Our Toes (p. 85). Originally written in English by the author and published in 2019 in *World Literature Today*.

Writing in Migration (p. 139). Both the Spanish version and English translation were first published in May 2020 in *Latin American Literature Today*.

The End of Women's Silence (p. 151). Both the Spanish version and English translation were first published in April 2019 in *Literal Magazine*.

Touching Is a Verb (p. 155). The Spanish version of this text was first published in the *Revista de la Universidad de México*, and the English translation was first published in *3:AM Magazine* on May 14, 2020.

More Translated Literature from the Feminist Press

Arid Dreams: Stories by Duanwad Pimwana, translated by Mui Poopoksakul

La Bastarda by Trifonia Melibea Obono, translated by Lawrence Schimel

Beijing Comrades by Bei Tong, translated by Scott E. Myers

Cockfight by María Fernanda Ampuero, translated by Frances Riddle

The Iliac Crest by Cristina Rivera Garza, translated by Sarah Booker

The Living Days by Ananda Devi, translated by Jeffrey Zuckerman

Mars: Stories by Asja Bakić, translated by Jennifer Zoble

Pretty Things by Virginie Despentes, translated by Emma Ramadan

The Restless by Gerty Dambury, translated by Judith G. Miller

Testo Junkie: Sex, Drugs, and Biopolitics in the Pharmacopornographic Era by Paul B. Preciado, translated by Bruce Benderson

Women Without Men by Shahrnush Parsipur, translated by Faridoun Farrokh

The Feminist Press publishes books that ignite movements and social transformation. Celebrating our legacy, we lift up insurgent and marginalized voices from around the world to build a more just future.

See our complete list of books at
feministpress.org

THE FEMINIST PRESS
AT THE CITY UNIVERSITY OF NEW YORK
FEMINISTPRESS.ORG